EX LIBRIS

THIS BOOK IS GIVEN
TO
THE CARDINGTON PUBLIC LIBRARY
IN LOVING MEMORY
OF

ELIZABETH CONAWAY WILSON

BY

REVEILLE CLUB

1987

THE
HISTORY OF
NEW
YORK
CITY

BILL HARRIS

Text and captions: Bill Harris
Designed by Design Box
Editorial: Gill Waugh and Pauline Graham
Archive Commissioning Editor: Andrew Preston
Photographic Research: Jean Gale and Leora Kahn
Production: Ruth Arthur, Joanna Keywood and David Proffit
Director of Publishing: David Gibbon
Director of Production: Gerald Hughes

Illustrations selected from the Bettmann Archive

CLB 2293
© 1989 Archive Publishing,
a division of Colour Library Books Ltd., Godalming, Surrey, England.
This 1989 edition published by Portland House,
a division of dilithium Press, Ltd.
distributed by Crown Publishers, Inc.,
225 Park Avenue South, New York, New York 10003
Printed and bound in Italy.
ISBN 0 517 68905 7
h g f e d c b a

Library of Congress Cataloging in Publication Data

Harris, Bill 1933
        History of New York City / Bill Harris
             p.   cm.
        ISBN 0 517 68905 7
         1. New York (N.Y.) – History.   I. Title.
   F128,3.H27 1989
     974.7'1 – dc20   89-8534
                                                                      CIP

THE
HISTORY OF
NEW
YORK
CITY

BILL HARRIS

PORTLAND HOUSE

CHAPTER	CONTENTS	

THE COMPANY TOWN

The 17th-century Dutch didn't need a colony in North America. They didn't even want one. And when Henry Hudson gave them a claim to the continent's greatest port, they considered his expedition a failure. For one thing, he hadn't followed their orders and then, to add insult to injury, he sailed back to his native England rather than to Holland. The English impounded his ship and her log vanished. As far as the Amsterdam merchants were concerned, they had been cheated out of eight hundred guilders.

The Dutch businessmen hired Hudson for the expedition because he had already taken two voyages in the direction of the Arctic Circle and convinced them he had come close to finding a route to the Indies across the top of the world. The Dutch already controlled the sea lanes to the East through their fortifications at the southern tip of Africa, and they didn't want any other country to have access to a back door if there happened to be one. In their bidding for Hudson's services, they came out ahead of the

When Henry Hudson sailed up the river in his ship Half Moon, *he thought he was going to find a passage to the riches of the East. Instead, he discovered the route to Albany. But he also discovered new riches in the skins of little creatures coveted back home, and a native population willing to sell them for beads and trinkets.*

The Half Moon *was a frail vessel, especially considering that the Dutch merchants who commissioned her expected Henry Hudson to sail to the Indies by way of the North Pole.*

competition by adding a clause to the contract that they would pay his wife an annuity if the master mariner didn't return within a year. Another clause was quite specific about where he should search for the Northwest Passage and instructed him to "think of no other routes." But Henry Hudson clearly had other things on his mind.

He headed north as ordered, but six weeks later he turned west. He said in his report that his crew refused to obey his orders to plunge ahead into the frozen north. But in the streets of Amsterdam it was whispered that he had been impressed by the maps and writings of his friend Captain John Smith, who had explored the North American coast and was sure there was a great river somewhere between Virginia and Canada that would lead to the other side. According to the gossip, Smith had also given Hudson a map, made by the Italian explorer Giovanni Verrazano eighty-five years earlier, that pinpointed exactly where such a river might be. If his crew had been less than cooperative

in helping him fulfill the terms of his Dutch contract, it's likely that Captain Hudson didn't really care. He doesn't seem to have been too concerned about business ethics, and any wild promise was worth making in return for a ship and a crew to follow a dream.

His ship, the *Half Moon*, arrived off Sandy Hook on September 2, 1609. The next morning, he spotted what looked like an open sea beyond the sandbar and, after exploring it for a few days, he found a wide river beyond. The natives were generally friendly, though crew members noted that they were sharp traders and "exceedingly adroit at carrying away whatever they took a fancy to." In an apparent attempt to find out what other vices they may be prone to, Hudson invited some of the chiefs aboard his ship and gave them "so much wine and aqua vitae that they were all merry." He reported that they found the experience strange and didn't know how to react to it. But they adapted well. The next day they were back with the makings

of a feast and an apparent craving for more merriment.

The scene was repeated many times as the *Half Moon* meandered up the river. Hudson must have been beside himself with joy. He felt he was on the verge of discovering the Holy Grail of explorers; the natives were friendly and the landscape the finest, he said, that he'd ever seen. But his joy was to be short lived. Instead of a route to the Indies, Henry Hudson had found the way to Albany.

Discouraged, he turned around and began making plans to go home. The return trip wasn't nearly as pleasant. On the way back down the river, an Indian who had made off with the captain's pillow and two of his shirts was shot for his trouble. The next day the *Half Moon's* crew shot a half-dozen red men on the shore, and then steered their ship for the open sea. Captain Hudson seems to have been in a foul mood.

At any rate, he was in no mood for a face-to-face interview with his employers, and set a course for England rather than Holland. He sent a terse report on

The natives were friendly when Hudson landed at Manhattan, and they got friendlier still when he brought out the firewater.

The ships of the Dutch West India Company began arriving in force after 1613, and going back to Holland loaded to the gunnels with beaver skins.

good money after bad. They had profitable enterprises in Indonesia to think about and were perfectly willing to forget about North America.

Amsterdam was at the center of world trade and finance at the beginning of the 17th century, and the Dutch East India Company was far from the only game in town. When a report on Hudson's expedition was finally published, some Dutch merchants were intrigued by the possibilities it suggested. What caught their eye was the fact that the river valley he explored abounded in beaver and that the natives seemed willing to sell their furs at low prices. It was an opportunity many Dutch merchants had been dreaming of. Until then, the French trappers in the St. Lawrence Valley had a monopoly on the beaver trade, and their best customers were the Dutch, who had access to lucrative markets in Germany and Russia. The Hudson Valley represented an opportunity to cut out the Gallic middlemen. The need seemed even more urgent because the Dutch merchants had recently developed a new use for beaver fur. Originally it had been used to make coats and capes, but after a season or two, the outer hairs fell off, leaving a rather ratty-looking coat. The accommodating Dutch bought the old garments back from their customers and recycled them as felt for hats. By 1613, beaver hats were so popular in Northern Europe that the need for a new source of the fur was almost desperate.

It was the year the Hudson River was rediscovered by Adriaen Block, a Dutch adventurer in search of furs. When his ship burned to the waterline, he and his crew became the first European residents of Manhattan. During their stay they also constructed the first American-built ship, which they used to explore Long Island Sound and the beaver-bearing creeks and inlets around it. After Block went home the following year with his holds filled with furs, a group of Amsterdam merchants secured a government monopoly to exploit the territory which their charter called New Netherland. It had been five years since Henry Hudson had broken his contract with them, but now the Dutch thought they had found a way to turn the loss into a profit.

However, the profits weren't earmarked for the original Dutch East India Company investors. In 1621, when Holland resumed its old war with Spain, the Dutch government chartered the competing West

to Amsterdam and asked them for more money. His request fell on deaf ears. Five months later he signed on with a British company to try again and was once more on the high seas, safe from Dutch wrath.

Had there really been a Northwest Passage, Henry Hudson would probably have been the man to find it. His 1610 voyage led him to discover the huge Canadian inland sea that became known as Hudson's Bay. But if he had an instinct for the sea, he didn't have a knack for dealing with people. Before he had a chance to explore the bay he had discovered, his crew mutinied and set him adrift in an open boat. He was never seen again, alive or dead.

There were no mourners in Amsterdam. The Dutch East India Company, which had financed Hudson's previous voyage, was rich enough to absorb the loss, but as solid businessmen, its stockholders didn't like it much, and they certainly weren't prepared to throw

India Company, which had trade rights in West Africa and North and South America. It was well-funded to provide an army and a navy powerful enough to eliminate the Spanish holdings in South America and the Caribbean and to claim their riches for Holland. Moreover, it was expected to be self-financing through the African slave trade. New Netherland, which wasn't mentioned in the charter, came under its control through an accident of geography.

The company sent colonists to the mouth of the Hudson River three years later. But there were no great crowds on the banks of the Zuyder Zee waiting to book passage to New Amsterdam. The old one was perfectly fine for the people who lived there. The first families that did make the trip were French-speaking Walloons from southern Belgium, refugees from the recent European wars. Their leader was Peter Minuit, who had served his Dutch masters well when he bought Manhattan Island from the Indians for trinkets worth sixty guilders. However, when he had the largest ship of its day built from local timber, the company's directors denounced him as extravagant and his career began a downhill slide. He was eventually recalled and Wouter Van Twiller, the nephew of one of the company's directors, was sent to make New Amsterdam a more profitable enterprise.

The Company was never fond of spending money, and there were some, raised eyebrows in the accounting department when Peter Minuit paid sixty Guilders for Manhattan Island in 1626.

Van Twiller had his work cut out for him. When he arrived in New Amsterdam, the colony had been all but abandoned. Many of the Walloons had gone home, and no one had come to replace them. The company wasn't at all interested in colonization and had stopped funding emigration in an effort to cut their expenses. A few of its directors, realizing that if there was no one in New Amsterdam to load beaver pelts onto their boats there wouldn't be any profits at all, petitioned the company to establish a Charter of Privileges and Exemptions. Under its terms, they could personally claim large tracts of land in exchange for funding colonists to live on them. They would be known as "patroons" (patrons), with feudal power over their sponsored settlers and the profits made from what they produced. The exemption to their privileges was that the fur trade was exclusively reserved for the Dutch West India Company.

On the whole the idea didn't work very well. But the most successful of the patroonships was established by diamond merchant Kiliaen Van Rensselaer, the new governor's uncle. He recruited the required number of colonists and sent them to an estate he established surrounding the Dutch settlement at Fort Orange, now known as Albany. Van Rensselaer's holdings covered more than a thousand square miles, a rather large farm by anybody's standards. But he was able to buy it at a good price from the Mohican Indians, who had just lost a war with their neighbors, the Mohawks, and were anxious to move to the Berkshires. Young Wouter, the governor, took good care of his Uncle Kiliaen. Among other things, he transferred ownership of all the company's livestock to the patroon.

For his part, Van Rensselaer had a genius for finding the right kind of people to emigrate to his Hudson River estate. They were mostly young, resilient, adventuresome and eager. Decades later, even after the British took over, the colony's most effective home-grown leaders were the children of the men hand-picked to guarantee the personal profits of Kiliaen Van Rensselaer. The other patroons apparently didn't understand the formula. In the face of meager

profits, most of them were soon anxious to move on and began giving up their holdings. Fifteen years after it was established, the colony of New Amsterdam had less than a thousand residents. Meanwhile, the English colonies that surrounded it were bursting at the seams and expanding in the direction of Dutch territory.

This worried the Dutch government, which gave the West India Company an ultimatum. The company was forced to choose between populating the colony or giving it up. On the theory that half a loaf is better than none, it gave up its fur monopoly. The population doubled in a matter of months. But all the newcomers were as profit-oriented as the company itself, and the people who were already there had been bitten by the same bug. No one did anything but hunt for beaver. Farmers left their fields, shopkeepers shuttered their stores, and every able-bodied man in the colony dedicated himself to getting rich and getting back to Holland as quickly as possible. The Indians who did the actual trapping were the key to the beaver trade, and settlers began arranging lavish feasts, possibly

America's first example of business entertaining, to encourage their loyalty. Others followed Henry Hudson's example and plied them with wine and aqua vitae.

The Indians were pleased with the attention, and happy to trade beaver skins for trinkets they thought they needed. But the expanding population was using up more and more of their land. In the old days they had been willing to sell property for next to nothing. It hadn't cost them anything, after all, and there was plenty of land to go around. But in the 1640s they had learned a little something about business, and some of them were beginning to think they had been cheated.

The colony had a new governor by then, Willem Kieft, a hard-nosed Dutchman with mandates to re-establish law and order and to make the colony profitable. He didn't accomplish either one, but he earned his place in the pantheon of political geniuses by attempting to solve both problems by taxing the Indians. When he arrived, the New Amsterdam fort was falling down in ruins. His theory was that a

Washington Irving wrote that Father Knickerbocker was "a brisk-looking old gentleman." An artist illustrating an early volume of his diary (facing page) obviously hadn't read it. One of the kinder things old Knickerbocker said about peg-legged Peter Stuyvesant (above) was that he possessed "a sovereign contempt of the sovereign people."

The Dutch had a good relationship with the Indians, but once in a while the red men made pointed protests over the price they were paid for beaver skins.

couldn't book passage huddled behind the tumbledown walls of Fort Amsterdam. The countryside was deserted and, worse from the company's point of view, the beaver trade dried up.

In his wisdom, Governor Kieft didn't attempt to negotiate with the Indians, but turned instead to his neighbors in New England. The next blow was struck in Connecticut, where combined Dutch and English forces wiped out an entire community of 800 Indians in a single night. And so it continued. Every ship bound for Holland was still filled to capacity with refugees and, over the winter of 1643, the population of New Amsterdam was reduced to 200. The West India Company, meanwhile, responded to the situation by saying that while they realized how terrible conditions must be, profits from New Netherland didn't justify the expense of helping them.

Finally, in August, 1645, four months after the company had decided to fire him, Kieft negotiated a truce with the Indians, and New Amsterdam was once again safe for commerce. But the job of rebuilding would take a tough man. The Dutch West India Company had found such a man in the person of a leathery, one-legged, no-nonsense Calvinist named Peter Stuyvesant.

Stuyvesant had no doubts that destiny had brought him to this place and that he had been preordained to meet the challenge. He may have been right, but when he finally arrived, in 1647, he must have known he was in trouble. According to one estimate, some eighteen different languages were spoken in New Amsterdam at the time. The people were all individualists, and respect for authority, the cornerstone of Stuyvesant's philosophy, simply didn't exist. But the new Director General was willing to take them on. His first order was that pigpens and privies should be in back of houses and not in the streets. Then he put a 9.00 pm curfew on drinking, and banned it completely on Sundays. He also encouraged the shipowners among them to cruise nearby waters in search of Spanish ships to plunder. His constituents ignored the first two commands, but worked hard to follow the third to the letter. There was grumbling when he put a tax on liquor to raise funds to rebuild the fort, but not the open warfare that had met Governor Kieft's tax on the Indians. And as he

shipshape fort would protect the Indians as well as the Dutch, and therefore they ought to help pay for it. The Indians naturally laughed off the idea, but Kieft responded that if they didn't pay up, he had ways of forcing them to.

The war developed slowly, with Indian raids and Dutch retaliations from Staten Island to the northern settlements. It wasn't good for the fur business, but it wasn't an all-out war either. Life went on and profits trickled in. Then in 1643, Dutch-armed Mohawks swept down the river, sending the southern tribes into retreat toward Manhattan. Kieft saw it as an opportunity and ordered a counterattack. His troops massacred every Indian man, woman and child they could find. But they couldn't find all of them, and thereafter no settler was safe. Every ship bound for the Netherlands was filled to capacity with refugees, and those who

When the English demanded the surrender of New Amsterdam, Peter Stuyvesant reacted by tearing their note into little pieces. He was forced to paste them back together and his iron-fisted rule fell in pieces.

promulgated more and more laws, he was met with more and more laughter and resentment. Less than a year after his arrival, he wrote to his masters in Amsterdam that "the people are very wild and loose in their morals." The only course of action, he suggested, was to work with the children and forget about the adults who were "so far depraved that they are ashamed to learn anything good." The company's directors didn't agree. They sent back a message that the problem was obviously that the Director General wasn't doing his job. "We expect Your Honor to amend all this," they concluded.

Stuyvesant's troubles in his own colony were the least of his problems. He was surrounded by English colonies, whose governors let him know he was less than welcome in their midst. The New Englanders resented that their ships stopping at Manhattan, which many did for no better reason than that their masters wanted to wet their whistles after layovers in the Puritan ports of Boston and Plymouth, were subject to tariffs on their cargoes. They also objected to the fact that the Dutch had established a good trade selling guns to the Indians, and kept it up even when the weapons were turned against their own people. But there was nothing Stuyvesant could do about any of that. He had been sent to the New World to show a profit. His morals were, if anything, more unimpeachable than those of his Puritan counterparts, but he served the pleasure of the Dutch West India Company. Their only concern was the almighty guilder.

Stuyvesant also had a problem with former governor Wouter Van Twiller, who had taken over his late uncle's estate at Rensselaerswyck. Operating from Amsterdam, where the real power was, Van Twiller and his managing agent extracted every possible stuiver from the property. They even established a fort on the river that prevented ships from reaching the company's trading post at Fort Orange, which they felt competed with their own interests. Stuyvesant met the problem head-on by deporting the estate's manager and establishing a new town on the river's west bank, which he called Beverwyck. It attracted a lot of the Rensselaer tenants, who freed themselves from the patroonship by moving across the river. Stuyvesant's troubles were far from over, but at least he was free for a while to concentrate on problems in Manhattan. There were plenty of them.

To make matters worse, there was a lawyer in their midst. Stuyvesant had agreed to govern with the advice of a council of nine citizens. One of the men he selected was a man with a law degree from the University of Utrecht. Adriaen Van der Donck was

The immigrants who settled New Amsterdam, like many of today's new arrivals, had one thing in mind: to make money and go back home ... as soon as possible.

In the beginning, Manhattan was an outpost of the real colony up the river at Fort Orange, now called Albany.

already well known as "the young patroon," the jonkheer whose former estate is now called Yonkers. He was also something of a Young Turk. From the day he was appointed to the council he began building a case to have the Director General recalled. When Stuyvesant got wind of it he fired not only Van der Donck but the other eight council members as well.

Prior to Stuyvesant's arrival, two local farmers who had been burned out in Indian raids brought charges against former Governor Kieft to recover their losses. The new Director General answered their charges by deporting them. But within days of dissolving the council, the two came back to haunt him with a full pardon from the Dutch States General. It caught Stuyvesant by surprise and he responded with a flash

of temper, tearing their pardon into little pieces. It was just the reaction Van der Donck needed. He circulated a petition and then left for the Netherlands with a strong request to have this wild man removed from their midst.

The States General was sympathetic and ordered reforms that included recalling Stuyvesant and giving the colony its own government. But the lawyer had a list of grievances against the Dutch West India Company, too. When he called for revoking its charter, the company's lobbyists went to work and not only watered down the rights he had secured for New Amsterdam, but turned Dutch public opinion against the colonists, whom they regarded as greedy, grasping ingrates. In spite of it, Van der Donck had gotten what he wanted. Peter Stuyvesant's days were numbered, and the colony would surely require the services of a lawyer to set up its new self-government.

It was a Pyrrhic victory. Before the attorney could go back to be carried up Broadway in triumph, Holland went to war with England, and the States General decided that Stuyvesant could be valuable in holding off the Puritans, who were closely allied with Oliver Cromwell, the enemy of the Dutch in London. They rescinded the Director General's recall and cancelled Van der Donck's passport. But they also let the order stand to establish a municipal government in New Amsterdam, which gave Stuyvesant the double power of representing the States General as well as the Dutch West India Company.

In return for the power, he was later forced to allow Jews, Quakers and even Lutherans into his colony, which didn't please him at all. But of all the European colonies in America, New Amsterdam had been the most tolerant from the very beginning, and tradition probably would have been served with or without Peter Stuyvesant. Without him, though, the English would certainly have moved in much sooner.

They had moved down from Massachusetts in 1636 and established a colony on the Connecticut River. Not long after, they crossed the Sound and expanded into another new colony on Long Island, right at New Amsterdam's door. The population of New England was ten times bigger than New Amsterdam's, and though Peter Stuyvesant had an enviable record as a

As well as New Amsterdam, the Dutch also had a thriving colony on Staten Island, which, according to some, was named by one of Henry Hudson's sailors when he asked the captain, "S'dat an island?" The truth of the matter is that it was named for the Staten-Generaal (States General) of the Dutch Republic.

There were dozens of Indian villages in Manhattan when Hudson first sailed by. But the one he visited was at the island's northern tip, on the shore of Spuyten Duyvil Creek.

soldier, he knew that diplomacy was the only way to keep the English where he thought they belonged. He negotiated a treaty with the New Englanders, giving them Connecticut above a line between Greenwich and Stamford, and Long Island east of a line drawn south from Oyster Bay. The pact also called for mutual assistance against the Indians.

Stuyvesant's masters in the Netherlands were still not too keen about using a portion of their profits to provide gunpowder for New Amsterdam, and the number of available able-bodied men wasn't growing as fast among the Dutch as among the New Englanders. But Stuyvesant was anything but a humble man and, through bluster and bombast, managed to keep the English at arm's length for nearly fifteen years after the treaty was signed. The fact that it held through three wars between Holland and England is another tribute to Stuyvesant's stubbornness as well as his diplomatic skills. But luck also had something to do with it.

At one stage, the war in Europe encouraged New Englanders to scheme to take over the Hudson Valley and the port at New Amsterdam. Finally, Cromwell himself joined the plot and sent a fleet of ships to Boston to mount an attack. But as they were being outfitted to sail down Long Island Sound, and as Long Islanders were arming themselves to join the battle, word arrived that a peace treaty had been signed between Britain and Holland three months earlier. The ships turned around and sailed instead to attack the French in Maine as though that had been their mission all along. Peter Stuyvesant was so grateful, he uncharacteristically appropriated enough funds to stage a celebration, including unlimited beer, for all the citizens of New Amsterdam.

They were pleased to have an excuse to celebrate, of course, but few of them cared one way or the other whether the English took over. Many were Englishmen who had slipped away from the restrictive life in the New England colonies, and most would have been happy to get out from under the influence of the Dutch West India Company. But there was another enemy in their midst that worried the traders among them and made the company directors furious. It was the Swedes, of all people.

New Amsterdam became New York on September 8, 1664, when Peter Stuyvesant gave the keys of the city to Colonel Richard Nichols in the name of England's Duke of York.

Sweden joined the rush to colonize North America in 1638. The order that went out from Stockholm called for no less than all of the continent to come under the domination of the Swedish Crown. It also specified that any places that had been given Dutch names should immediately be translated into Swedish. National pride had something to do with it, so did a longstanding rivalry between Sweden and the Netherlands. But the real motivating force behind the venture was a promoter named William Usselinx.

Usselinx had been one of the original founders of the Dutch West India Company. But he had a falling-out with his partners early in the game over whether the company should be run by its board of directors or by stockholder-colonists. The board of directors won. Undaunted, Usselinx sold his shares and took his ideas to Stockholm. In today's world, he would be accused of corporate espionage because he left Amsterdam armed with maps and charts and company reports on the southern reaches of New Netherland, an abandoned fort near the mouth of the Delaware River. English farmers had moved into the area from Virginia, as had the Dutch from further north. But though the Dutch West India Company said it owned the territory, it paid almost no attention to it.

The Company sat up and took notice when a pair of Swedish ships sailed up the Delaware. The expedition's leader requested permission from local farmers to put ashore to fill his water kegs, and when permission was granted, he took command of the abandoned fort, reconstructed it, renamed it Fort Christina and declared it the capital of New Sweden. To add insult to the injury, its commander turned out to be Peter Minuit, the same man who had established New Amsterdam a dozen years earlier. His new colony had twenty-three citizens – one Swede and twenty-two Dutchmen.

The next meeting of the Board of Directors of the Dutch West India Company is better left to to the imagination.

The Swedish company, meanwhile, launched a promotion campaign to encourage settlement in its new colony. But their pamphlets and oratory were largely ignored. The Swedes were no more interested in leaving home than the Dutch had been.

CHAPTER 1

New Amsterdam was a primitive place, but the work ethic that the Dutch brought with them ensured that the seeds of its commercial future were sown from the start.

Dutch officials didn't seem interested, either. Little was done about New Sweden for another seventeen years. Then, in 1655, a ship and two hundred soldiers were dispatched from Amsterdam. The force was augmented with a half-dozen other ships and about four hundred New Amsterdam volunteers. On September 5, the little fleet, commanded by Peter Stuyvesant, set sail for the Delaware River.

It was an easy victory for Stuyvesant. By the 24th, New Sweden had ceased to exist and was, once and for all it seemed, part and parcel of New Netherland. The West India Company, apparently more in need of funds than usual, sold the territory that Peter Minuit had originally bought for them from the Indians for a copper pot, to the City of Amsterdam for seven hundred thousand guilders. However, the new owners had no better luck in encouraging new settlement there than had the company or the Swedes.

September 1655 should have been a red-letter month for New Netherland. It had removed a competitor from its midst and shown the English that it knew how to fight. Instead, they were among the darkest days the colony had yet seen.

The Dutch fleet had no sooner left Manhattan to take on the Swedes than the Hudson River Indian tribes decided to join forces and go out to Eastern Long Island to subdue their cousins, the Montauks. Nearly two thousand of them converged at the northern end of Manhattan on the night of September 14. When they helped themselves to some of the apples from Hendrick Van Dyck's orchard, he responded by killing one of them, and at that moment the war party decided to postpone its trip to Long Island.

The next night they moved on the settlement, ransacking some houses and burning others, looking, they said, for Mynheer Van Dyck. The following morning it transpired that the only casualties were among the Indians themselves. They hadn't found the killer they were looking for, but they did find enough beer and rum to result in some monumental hangovers. The Europeans, on the other hand, were quite sobered by the experience. They had lived peacefully with the Indians for several years by then, but they had never seen so many of them in New Amsterdam at one time.

Most of their able-bodied men were off fighting the Swedes, their city was in ruins and that huge war party was still lurking in upper Manhattan.

The Indian chiefs apologized and promised to move on. They said they were on their way to Long Island and had no reason to stay. The Dutch relaxed and broke out the brandy to celebrate their deliverance. The Indians, meanwhile, had also accumulated a good supply of liquor and spent the day sipping it and wondering among themselves how Van Dyck had slipped through their fingers. They found him late in the day, but he managed to escape to the fort with one of their arrows in his back.

Witnesses later said that the entire garrison was drunk by then and, indeed, there doesn't seem to be any other explanation as to why its commander ordered his woefully outnumbered men to attack the Indians. Or why they did it with such enthusiasm. The Indians were startled and backed off that night. But in the cold light of dawn they forgot their mission against the Montauks. The enemy, it seemed, was right here in Manhattan.

They destroyed settlements on the west side of the Hudson as well as farms on Staten Island and Manhattan. Dozens of New Netherlanders were killed, hundreds were taken prisoner and held for ransom. Cattle were slaughtered, newly harvested crops destroyed and the whole colony terrorized. Peter Stuyvesant, who had hoped to come home in triumph from New Sweden, came home to a defeated people.

But he wasn't a man who understood defeat. Even before he stepped ashore, he had drawn up a plan to strengthen the wall he had built at the northern end of New Amsterdam to keep the English out, and he spent the next several days negotiating with the Indians over the return of the hostages they were holding. His critics said he should take a few hostages himself, but he refused, which made negotiating a peace treaty with the red men a good deal easier.

By spring, the days of September were nothing more than an unpleasant memory. The principal topic of conversation in local taverns that winter had been where to place the blame for the Indian raids. Manhattanites were about equally divided between

The industrious Dutch quickly turned the tip of Manhattan into a bustling little city with a sturdy fort, windmills, canals and other touches of home, including a gibbet – a not-so-subtle reminder that the inhabitants should behave.

Stuyvesant, never anything less than a company man, began to take his responsibilities as a representative of the States General more seriously and started running New Amsterdam as a colony as well as as a trading post. The people of New Netherland were never overly fond of their Director General, but, for all his faults, no one ever questioned his honesty. As he began encouraging them to think of America as their home, they responded and the colony began to prosper again. They were slow to obey his laws, and cheating the company was still their favorite game, but they were united for the first time and most had decided that their own future was tied to the future of

The city's Seal includes a Dutch windmill and the sources of its early wealth: barrels of flour and beavers. The date refers to the colony's change to New York, whose Latin name appears on the Seal.

accusing the English or the Swedes for starting it all. Very few blamed Demon Rum for the way it turned out. Peter Stuyvesant himself told them that the tragedy had been visited on them by God as punishment for their sins, which were, indeed, legion. He railed at them for their drunkenness, their profanity and their generally uncivilized treatment of the Indians as well as of each other. And he gave them new laws designed to curb their instincts. As usual, the laws weren't obeyed. But his determination seems to have impressed the red men, who never bothered New Amsterdam again.

New Netherland. But its days as a Dutch colony were numbered.

By 1660, when the biggest problem the New Amsterdamers faced was inflation brought on by prosperity, an Englishman who had been living in Holland went home to London to restore the monarchy. As Charles II, he would eventually repay the Dutch for their hospitality by annexing their American colonies. The English in America had been doing everything they could to take over New Amsterdam and, at various times, seemed close to succeeding. Stuyvesant was convinced the new King would finally make it possible. But when he petitioned both the company and the States General to help him build his defenses, they responded that the new English King was a friend of theirs, and besides, they couldn't afford to outfit the soldiers they had already sent, let alone send new ones. At the same time, they ordered him to take back the parts of Long Island and Connecticut he had given away. And they suggested that since the Indians had calmed down and the English King was obviously friendly, it might be a good time to cut down the size of his defense force as a means of cutting expenses.

Then, in 1664, the English King gave his brother, the Duke of York, all the territory in North America between the Delaware and Connecticut rivers. On

When the British sailed into the harbor to take charge, New Amsterdam was a thriving prize worth taking.

CHAPTER 1

Not much changed but the name after the English moved into New Amsterdam, except that the ships in the harbor had a different destination in Europe.

August 28, four British warships sailed into New Amsterdam harbor to claim the gift formally. Stuyvesant's first instinct was to fight back, in spite of the fact that there were less than six hundred pounds of powder in the fort. He sent messages to Rensselaerswyick and the Long Island settlements asking for help, but was told that they had barely enough men and firepower to protect themselves. The English, meanwhile, put two thousand troops ashore in Brooklyn and sent a delegation to New Amsterdam with surrender terms. They were generous terms, promising to change nothing in the lives and liberties of the people, and to provide complete protection, but under a new master, the King of England.

However, for all the problems it had given him, Peter Stuyvesant's master was still the Dutch West India Company and he was prepared to defend its interests to the death. When the burgomasters asked to see the document the English had sent, the Director General tore it to pieces. The people outside were on the verge of rioting and when they sent a delegation to demand that Stuyvesant show them the letter, he was forced to collect the scraps and have them pasted together. It had no sooner been translated from

English into Dutch than Stuyvesant was handed a petition from his own people demanding surrender. On September 8, 1664, New Amsterdam became known as New York.

Very little else changed and life went on much as usual. Peter Stuyvesant, the company man, was stripped of his authority. But even though he was technically still Director General of the West India Company's colony at Curaçao, he chose to stay on and retire to his Manhattan farm. The members of his governing council, most of whom kept their jobs in the new English government, drafted a letter to the company's directors in Amsterdam that put their real feelings on the line by saying the recent turn of events "happened in consequence of your Honors' neglect and forgetfulness." The company responded by bringing charges against Stuyvesant for having "always paid more attention to the people's particular affairs than to the company's interest."

Stuyvesant spent three years in Holland defending himself. The States General finally let the case die in committee and the former Director General of New Amsterdam was allowed to go home again. He was a New Yorker for the rest of his life.

Peter Stuyvesant, who surrendered more to the pleading of his people than to the threat of English guns, stayed in New York, in spite of the change, for the rest of his life.

ENGLISH AS A SECOND LANGUAGE

In 1760, as New Yorkers were preparing for the centennial celebration of English acquisition, a Manhattan matron wrote in her diary that "the English language is beginning to be more generally understood here." The old Dutch patroons had prospered since 1664 under new patents that required them to pay rent to the Duke of York and his heirs. Britain provided them with a new market, and trade with Holland continued over English objections after Peter Stuyvesant intervened and convinced them that the Indians preferred Dutch trade goods to English imports. When a Dutch fleet retook the colony in 1673, residents were just as happy to hear, a year later, that the territory the Dutch had renamed New Orange had been negotiated back to the British in exchange for Surinam. During that year, the West India Company made a demand that all customs duties previously collected by the British from Amsterdam-bound ships, should be paid into its treasury. The demand was ignored and the company declared bankruptcy. Not a tear was shed anywhere in New York.

Some of the fortune hunters went back to Holland after the British took over, but most stayed and they were joined by French, German, Scandinavian and Dutch as well as English settlers, all of whom were attracted to New York because the wilderness had been cleared and the Indians were friendly. But if an English flag flew over the fort at the tip of Manhattan, life in New York still had a strong Dutch accent. Its aristocracy, made up of successful businessmen, was almost completely Dutch and, thanks to them, the city became the crown jewel of the colony. In Holland, unlike other European countries, including England, city life was run by merchant classes made up of people who didn't move to country estates at the first sign of prosperity. This made New York unusual in America, too. Leaders in the other colonial cities were churchmen or politicians, but in New York they were businessmen first and only became involved in political affairs as a means of improving the quality of city life, not to mention the climate for business. They were careful to let the English think they were subservient to London, but they managed to make sure that the bulk of the profits stayed in New York.

When the Duke of York was given the territory, his advisers estimated that it would enhance his income by £30,000 a year. But, like others, he soon discovered there was a big difference between being the lord of an English manor and the proprietor of an English colony. New Yorkers, he found, weren't simple farmers and craftsmen, but crafty men who had developed an unusually creative approach to bookkeeping.

The Duke had also made the mistake of giving the territory west of the Hudson River to his friends Sir John Berkeley and Sir George Carteret. They named it New Jersey, and sent a representative to organize things. When the interloper arrived, New York's Governor Nicholls was horrified. He sent off a strong letter to London saying that New York needed to control the whole of its harbor and both sides of the river. But when the Duke tried to exchange his gift for land further south, he was informed that it was too late. Nicholls predicted that New York and New Jersey would eventually destroy each other, but he was ordered to help the new proprietors establish a colony across the bay at Elizabethtown. It would become a thorn in the side of every colonial governor of New York. It also taught the Duke of York a lesson about generosity, a quality he rarely displayed ever again. He hoped to recapture New Jersey when his patent was renewed after the 1674 treaty with the Dutch, but Carteret had anticipated him and reached the King first to have his own rights confirmed.

The Duke also hoped that his new patent would change things to his advantage in New York. The former New Amsterdamers had relied on the terms of their original surrender to maintain their old rights, which made them a good deal less governable from the English point of view. But the new treaty contained a clause spelling out rights and privileges for New Yorkers "in the same manner as before the rupture." To the Duke and his minions, that meant they still had a license to carry on "the illicit trade with Holland." There was no profit in that, either for the Duke or the English merchants.

In 1679, Edmund Andros, the Duke's Governor, reported to London that the twenty-four towns and villages of the former New Netherland and the estates surrounding them were valued at £150,000. But the

CHAPTER 2

Previous page: H.R.H. the Duke of York, the future King James II of England. Below: even as late as 1790, when the British colony had become an American city, the Dutch influence was still part of the skyline.

Duke himself was required to fork out over £1,100 in the same year to keep his province functioning. A half dozen years later, when the Duke became James II, the last of the Stuart kings, New York became a royal province and the problems of profit and loss became the responsibility of the Committee for Trade and Plantations. But, as had been the case right from the start, New Yorkers doggedly stuck to the philosophy that charity begins at home.

Among the men who kept their profits to themselves was Frederick Philipse, whose £13,000 fortune made him one of the richest men in America, if not the entire British Empire. Like so many of his fellow New Yorkers, and those who would follow in their footsteps, he was a self-made man with a special knack for making money.

Philipse arrived in New Amsterdam in the 1650s as a carpenter, and within a few years had accumulated enough money to charter a West India Company ship to begin a coastal trade with the Virginia colony. He

earned the funds by secretly buying wampum, the official legal tender of New Amsterdam, directly from the Indians and hoarding it. By creating a money shortage, he was able to fix the rate of exchange for guilders and, eventually, accumulated enough of them to pay cash for a house in Manhattan, as well as buying the former country estate of Peter Stuyvesant's old Nemesis, Adriaen Van der Donck. After he became a trader, Philipse expanded quickly, built his own ships and established a trade with the Indians as well as the English. He increased his fortune and the potential for making it grow when he married a rich widow, Margaret Hardenbroek De Vries, who was herself well established as a trader and ship owner; one of two women who were ranked among the richest merchants in New Amsterdam. After the British took over, she kept up her bustling trade with Holland and refused to pay English customs duties on the grounds that her ships flew the Dutch flag. It took the authorities more than a dozen years to disabuse her of the notion.

Her husband, meanwhile, had joined a great many local businessmen in finding the perfect way of avoiding customs taxes. Their ships picked up cargoes by attacking other ships on the high seas and then landed the untaxed merchandise on the eastern end of Long Island, bringing it overland into Manhattan under the noses of the tax collectors. Today we call them pirates, but they called themselves privateers. It was said that Philipse built a port on the Island of Madagascar as a pirate rendezvous, and routinely shared in the proceeds of their cargoes. At home he was a solid citizen, though, active in the political and social life of the colony. But then, so were the other pirates of 17th century New York. Among them was Henry Morgan, whose descendant, J. Pierpont Morgan, would one day name his yacht after the buccaneer's ship. Old Henry had developed a facade of respectability and ended his days as Governor of the Island of Jamaica, which entitled him to be buried with a state funeral. On the other hand, Captain William Kidd, the best remembered of the New York pirates, came to a more ignominious end. At home in New York, Kidd was highly regarded as a merchant and well known as a philanthropist. On the high seas, though, he had a quite different reputation. None of his neighbors really cared where his money came from, and local representatives of His Majesty's Government, some of whom were on the Captain's

Though the English tried to change them, the New Amsterdam surrender treaty promised the Dutch that they could go on living as before. They did. With pleasure.

CHAPTER 2

Merchantmen calling at 17th-century New York found it a very profitable port of call. Sailors found it a nice place to visit, too, even if their captains often resorted to unusual hangover cures when it was time to hoist their sails again. A well-respected New York merchant, shipowner and philanthropist, Captain Kidd is better remembered for his piratical exploits on the high seas. The illustration shows him putting paid to his gunner, Thomas Moore.

payroll, cared even less. But they all responded in horror when Kidd attacked a fleet of English merchant ships in the Mediterranean. He was hunted down and hanged in London for his effrontery. To this day, people regularly poke around Long Island beaches looking for the fabulous treasure the Captain was alleged to have left behind. But it is more likely to have been left in the pockets of officials on both sides of the Atlantic whom Kidd accused of making him a tool of their own "ambition and avarice."

There was plenty of both in the City of New York, and the business community had stumbled on a perfect way to satisfy its lust for riches. The Dutch farmers who had settled the Hudson Valley were the most skilful in America and, in 1676, when other colonies were short of grain, New York had a surplus. Governor Edmund Andros decreed that the local price should be raised to be on a par with the rest of the colonies and set new standards for the manufacture of flour. He had previously given the businessmen of Albany exclusive rights in trading with Indians and,

even though the value of beaver skins was dropping, the Manhattan business community had been lobbying for a special privilege of its own. The Governor responded in 1680 with a law that said no inland city in the province could engage in overseas trade and gave New York City the exclusive right to sift flour and pack it for export either abroad or to any of the other colonies. The monopoly, which lasted nearly twenty years, dramatically increased the wealth of the city, and local real estate prices increased to ten times their old value in the last few years of the century. More than six hundred new houses were built in Manhattan, and it became the boom town its founders had dreamed of. Of course, they had been dreaming of beavers, not bread.

Over the next century, the province was ruled by a succession of governors selected from among the favorites at the English Court, and they generally ranged from bad to worse. The city prospered in spite of them. Possibly the most infamous of the lot was Lord Cornbury, who served between 1702 and 1708.

In spite of its prosperity, no one would have believed what the port of New York would become a century later.

CHAPTER 2

His High Mightiness was born Edward Hyde, the son of the Earl of Clarendon and a cousin of Queen Anne, who appointed him to his exalted position. When he arrived in New York, he was given a hero's welcome because the people felt that as a relative of the Queen, he would have her ear and could help enhance their position in the Empire. But the new Governor had another ear on his mind.

The city leaders entertained Cornbury and his wife at a lavish banquet a few days after they arrived, in hopes that he would explain his policies and goals in his after-dinner speech. But when the hour arrived, the speech was devoted entirely to the great beauty of Lady Cornbury. She had the most beautiful ears in the Empire, he told them, and he commanded everyone in the room to walk through a receiving line and feel Her Ladyship's ears for themselves. A week later the Cornburys invited the local aristocracy to a gala ball at the governor's mansion. Many stayed home, not because they wanted to avoid more physical contact with the Governor's wife, but because His High Mightiness had included an admission charge in the invitation. Those who didn't respond were assessed a

Back in England, men like the Earl of Clarendon (above) grew fat on the New York trade. But a lot of the profits stayed in New York itself (right), where life was nearly as fine as in London itself.

special tax to cover the cost of admission they had hoped to avoid.

Ordinary citizens began to notice the new Governor the night he rode his horse into the King's Arms Tavern, ordered a whiskey for himself and water for the animal and then, when they both had had enough, he clattered out again, knocking over tables and chairs. But no one had seen anything yet.

Everyone in town knew they were in deep trouble the day Lord Cornbury appeared on Broadway wearing his wife's clothes. After several such appearances, he finally explained that it was no mere affectation but, since he represented a Queen, it was only fitting that he should dress like one. He also noted that he resembled Queen Anne anyway, even in his own clothes; a not so subtle reminder that she was his kinswoman.

The relationship stood him in good stead when he needed money, which was all of the time. No one in the city with money to spare hesitated to loan it to the Governor. Often he repaid them with generous grants of public land, the most generous of which was a huge tract, several miles along the Hudson, renamed Hyde

Clarendon's gift to New York was his son, the Royal Governor, Lord Cornbury (left), who often wore women's clothes because he felt he should look the part of the Queen's representative.

In spite of Kings and Queens, and Royal Governors, the city prospered under English rule and expanded far beyond the wall the Dutch had built to keep them out.

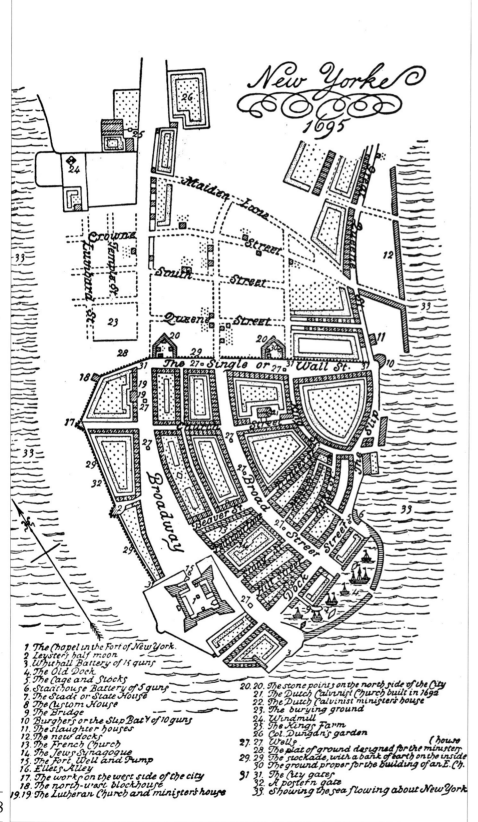

New Yorke 1695

1. The Chapel in the Fort of New York.
2. Leyster's half moon
3. Whithall Battery of 15 guns
4. The Old Dock
5. The Cage and Stocks
6. Stadthouse Battery of 5 guns
7. The Stadt or State House
8. The Custom House
9. The Bridge
10. Burghers or the Slip Bat.y of 10 guns
11. The slaughter houses
12. The new docks
13. The French Church
14. The Jews Synagogue
15. The Fort, Well and Pump
16. Ellets Alley
17. The works on the west side of the city
18. The north-west blockhouse
19.19. The Lutheran Church and ministers house

20.20. The stone points on the north side of the City
21. The Dutch Calvinist Church built in 1692
22. The Dutch Calvinist minister's house
23. The burying ground
24. Windmill
25. The Kings Farm
26. Col. Dungdn's garden
27.27. Wells
28. The plat of ground designed for the ministers (house
29.29. The stockade, with a bank of earth on the inside
30. The ground proper for the building of an E. Ch.
31.31. The City gates
32. A postern gate
33. Showing the sea flowing about New York

Park by its grateful new owners in honor of Cornbury's family. His Lordship also lined his pockets with public funds. In 1703 he informed the General Assembly that a French fleet was about to attack New York and requested funds to assemble a battery at the harbor entrance. But instead of building a fort, he used the money they gave him to build a country house for himself. When the local officials accused him of misappropriating their funds, he pointed out that since no French fleet had arrived in the harbor, the purpose of the appropriation must have been accomplished.

It wasn't as though the Cornburys didn't know how to save money. Not long after her arrival, Her Ladyship let it be known that she intended to improve the status of a backward colonial city by instituting a court similar to the Queen's in London. Several daughters of the city's best families were selected to be her ladies-in-waiting and were invited to live in the governor's mansion. The honor ended at the door when the young women discovered that the servants had been fired and they were to become their replacements. Lady Cornbury also had a habit of visiting the homes

of her subjects and stealing artifacts that caught her eye. She never kept anything, though. Usually within a few days she would sell what she had taken back to the original owner at prices reflecting the enhanced value of an item that had graced the governor's mansion.

The citizens of New York finally sent a petition to the Queen demanding a new governor, preferably not a royal relative. Cornbury was intercepted by his creditors as he attempted to board a London-bound ship and was thrown into debtors prison. He was finally released and sent back home when his father died nearly a year later and left him an estate large enough to cover his American debts.

The Governor who replaced him, General Robert Hunter, left his impression on his subjects when he sent a report back to England that concluded: "The Colonies are infants at their mother's breast, but such as will wean themselves when they become of age." It was food for thought. In another fifty years, some New Yorkers began to think they had, indeed, "become of age."

The Dutch had established a suburb several miles above New Amsterdam and named it Haarlem for a suburb of old Amsterdam. In the days of the English colony, it became a summer resort.

WHAT DID YOU DO DURING THE WAR?

On July 4, 1976, more than 125 sailing ships from all over the world converged on New York Harbor to mark the Bicentennial of America's Independence. On July 4, 1776, the largest fleet of hostile ships ever seen on the North American coast – 113 British men of war and transports – were anchored just beyond the Narrows. Their commander, General William Howe, had landed troops in Brooklyn and on Staten Island, and he was patiently waiting for his brother Richard, Admiral Viscount Howe, to arrive with 150 more ships and 2,500 fresh fighting men.

When General George Washington, who was headquartered in Manhattan at the time, ordered the Declaration of Independence to be read to his Continental Army on July 9, there were no ringing church bells, firing cannons, blazing bonfires or any of the other displays of enthusiasm that welcomed the news in other American cities. New Yorkers were terrified that any sudden noises might be taken as a signal for the British cannons to begin firing. Many of

them also had mixed emotions about what the Continental Congress had done in Philadelphia. In fact, New York's delegation was the only one that had abstained from voting for it. On that same day, July 9, it agreed to go along with the others, and the title of the document was changed to become "The Unanimous Declaration of the Thirteen United States of America."

It was out of character for New Yorkers not to take advantage of any opportunity for a celebration. The preceding April, when news reached the city that British soldiers had fired on the Americans at Lexington and Concord in Massachusetts, and that the Americans had given a good account of themselves, New York's party lasted for three days and, before the smoke from the bonfires had cleared, New Yorkers had sent a half ton of gunpowder, nearly all they had, to Boston. It left them vulnerable to any British warship and, to punctuate the possibility, His Majesty's battleship *Asia* was anchored off Governor's Island with sixty-four cannons aimed at the city.

New Yorkers had dumped tea into the harbor to protest the British stamp taxes, just as their Boston brethren had done. They had raised Liberty Poles, harassed Tories and established their own Provincial Congress in defiance of the British Governor and his Council. But they had not stopped drinking tea, nor

When American Minutemen faced the British at Concord Bridge in '75, New Yorkers were faced with British warships in the harbor.

tarred and feathered anyone loyal to the Crown. And most of them sincerely liked and respected the Royal Governor, William Tryon. There were radicals at both ends of the scale, but most New Yorkers were convinced that the whole affair would eventually blow over and they could get on with their business. Most had good reason to want to maintain the status quo. As one of them had written when the winds of revolution began blowing in New England, "Our colony is extending its trade, encouraging the arts and sciences and cultivating its lands. Its inhabitants are daily increasing in riches, in wealth and opulence."

But once the shooting began, it wasn't easy to steer a middle course. The Continental Congress commissioned George Washington as Commander in Chief of its army and, on June 25, 1775, he was scheduled to pass through New York on his way to take charge at Boston. The city felt obliged to give him a welcome and a strong show of support. But at the same hour he was scheduled to arrive, Governor Tryon was coming back from a long visit to England, and New York felt compelled to give him an official welcome, too. Then, as now, it was a city that loved a parade, but two at the same time was a little more than even it could handle.

There were ten companies of uniformed soldiers in Manhattan at the time, so it was decided to dispatch one of them to the northern part of the city, where Washington and his party would be welcomed after having been met in New Jersey and diplomatically detoured. A second company was stationed at the East River pier, where the Governor would land, and the other eight were assembled in the middle ready to march in the direction of whichever VIP arrived first. Fortunately for protocol, Tryon had been warned of the dilemma and decided to hold his ship in the harbor for four hours to give them a chance to honor General Washington. The General's parade ended minutes before the Governor landed, but there was time enough for the crowd to reassemble across town for the second celebration of a very long day. The city had successfully placed its feet in both camps.

At least it thought it had. People who were beginning to matter in the other twelve colonies viewed New Yorkers with almost the same animosity they felt for Londoners. Politics aside, they were convinced that New York was the most sin-ridden city on the North

American continent. There were brothels in the City of Brotherly Love, and it was estimated that there was a tavern in every eighth building in Boston, but New York had more of both than either city. Americans from the Carolinas to Maine continually castigated New Yorkers for not being "church people." This despite the fact that there were seventeen churches in less than a square mile of Manhattan, including a Quaker meeting house and a synagogue, and Catholic Mass was said every Sunday in private houses. The problem was not so much that they didn't go to church, but that they went to too many different kinds of churches. To other colonials, that was vaguely un-American. And, to add insult to injury, New York was open for business every Sunday. On the way home from church, a woman could shop for the latest fashions, and her husband could wait for her in a convenient tavern.

To people in the other colonies thinking of freedom and eager to fight for liberty, New Yorkers were despised as freethinkers and libertines. Most assuredly,

in the opinion of most Americans, they were not to be trusted.

As if to prove they were right, New York had difficulty recruiting the three-thousand soldiers requested by the Continental Congress. Some young men flatly refused and others ran off to join the other side. The city had to borrow troops from Connecticut to defend itself against a possible attack. By midsummer, though, enough local boys had signed up to allow the Connecticut soldiers to go home again. But the New York regiments quickly left town too, on a mission to end British control in Canada. Meanwhile, the enemy battleship in the harbor had been joined by a second warship. But everybody in Manhattan knew that just one would have enough firepower to burn the city to the ground, no matter how many soldiers were billeted there. Not a shot had been fired, but New York considered itself to be a city under siege.

Ordinarily, the classic plan of a siege is to starve the inhabitants into surrender. In this case, the besieged had an opportunity to turn the tables, but that didn't

During the British occupation, prisoners of war were kept in the Rhinelander Sugar House (facing page), a small section of which still stands in Police Plaza.

Through most of the war years, the waterfront markets were the scene of the real action in New York. After all, the enemy was armed with pound sterling. It was an opportunity too good to miss.

make good business sense. There were hundreds of hungry sailors out there in the harbor, and dozens of small boats regularly ferried back and forth with all the meat and cheese, beer and wine and other supplies the British were willing to pay for. One enterprising businessman even set up a water-borne laundry service so the officers could keep up proper appearances.

Not everyone in the city approved of consorting with the enemy. There was a rash of thefts from His Majesty's Manhattan storehouses, and local merchants loyally abided by the Continental ban on English imports. Traditionally, the bulk of their profits came from the Caribbean trade anyway, but not having the luxuries they had become used to cast a pall over New York's mood and nudged a great many former Tories and indifferent citizens over into the rebel camp. Governor Tryon responded by taking up residence on a merchant ship in the harbor and running his government from there. The Provincial Congress concerned itself with punishing British sympathizers, and the overflow of prisoners filled jails as far up the river as Kingston.

In spite of its attempts to rout the royalists, New York still had a poor reputation among the other colonies and, after the city's cannons were destroyed by persons unknown on a cold January night in 1776, General Charles Lee decided to take matters into his own hands. Lee, a senior adviser to General Washington, was a noted Tory-baiter and just as well known for his opinion that New Yorkers, even the patriots among them, were beneath contempt. He had no trouble finding like-minded men in Connecticut, and together they marched on Manhattan. Most of his soldiers had the impression that their mission was to destroy New York, and the New Yorkers knew that Lee would probably encourage them. The soldiers had no sooner arrived from the north than a twenty-four-gun British frigate sailed into the harbor from the other direction. No one knew her intentions.

The result was fear. And something many 20th century New Yorkers still fear: gridlock. Everyone who could afford it had one thing in mind: to get out of town. Every street in the city was filled with wagons headed for the docks. Empty wagons were soon on their way back for fresh loads and, within an hour or two, none of them was able to move in either direction. It was a useless adventure anyway. There were no available boats to take anyone off the island. The traffic

jam lasted through the night and well into the next afternoon when suddenly people began to notice something strange. The British guns were silent.

The ship's commander, Sir Henry Clinton, sent a message to the mayor that this was strictly a social call on his old friend Governor Tryon. Most people didn't believe him, least of all General Lee, who ordered fresh troops from Westchester and New Jersey and ordered the local Committee of Safety to prepare lodging for 5,000 men. The city's entire population at the time was only about 20,000, which made the request a staggering logistical problem. Meanwhile, the Connecticut contingent, already in town, asked to be relieved of its duty. They had come to burn New York to the ground, not protect it. Permission was granted and they rode off in the direction of their farms.

Lee put his new troops to work building fortifications and spent his own time trying to convince the citizens of New York that Governor Tryon was a representative of the enemy. Neither project was very successful. Work progressed slowly on the forts, partly because of the frozen ground, but just as much because the Colonial Army he had brought to town had almost as many officers, who supervised rather than worked, as enlisted men, who weren't too enthusiastic about fortifying a city they ranked on a par with Sodom and Gomorrah. Lee's whispering campaign against the Royal Governor got nowhere at all. Tryon commanded a half-dozen ships out there in the harbor and he paid for their provisions in English pounds sterling. Lee paid for his supplies in Continental dollars.

Lee's soldiers also made themselves unpopular by what seemed to be a maniacal determination to cut down every tree in Manhattan. The winter of '75-'76 was one of the coldest ever recorded in the New York area, and they simply wanted to keep warm. Manhattanites, who had always imported firewood from surrounding counties, were horrified to see their apple orchards, not to mention next year's supply of hard cider, being systematically destroyed. Street trees, including the elms that had lined Broadway until then, were all cut down and never replaced. It made New Yorkers begin to wonder if independence was really worth it.

But if they harbored any secret love for the British, they didn't show it. After the American defeat at Quebec, the Continental Congress sent out an order for a new army to march on Canada. New York's quota was nearly the same as the one it had so much trouble meeting the previous year, but this time they rushed to fill it and, in the early spring, the required number, and more, were headed north.

They had no sooner left than word came from Boston that General Howe and his British troops had pulled up stakes and left town, probably on their way to New York. Lee was reassigned to Virginia, and General Washington was making preparations to march his main army to New York. The stage, apparently, was set.

The vanguard of the Continental Army arrived at the end of March, bringing with it the promise of 10,000 more troops to follow. Combined with the 3,000 already in Manhattan and 8,000 others on the way from the south and west, the military population would outnumber civilians, who weren't at all sure whether that was to be a blessing or a curse. Storekeepers and tavern owners, on the other hand, were delighted.

The new troops were commanded by General Israel Putnam of Connecticut, who was speechless when he arrived to find that New Yorkers were still routinely supplying the British ships in the harbor and that the city's leaders regularly sailed out for friendly meetings with the Royal Governor. When he saw British sailors playing ball on Governor's Island, he nearly had apoplexy. After issuing an order to stop trading and communicating with the enemy, he put a thousand men to work under cover of darkness digging trenches and building breastworks on the island. When the sun rose the next morning, all of the British ships had left the harbor. They hadn't gone any further than Gravesend Bay in Brooklyn, but Putnam had made his point and he was pleased to report to the Continental Congress that hostilities had commenced in the City of New York.

General Washington himself arrived a few days later. But if hostilities had broken out, there was no sign of it. He had plenty of time to get to know the city

From November 1776, until they finally left in November 1783, British soldiers regularly marched in the streets of New York.

CHAPTER 3

and the people who ran it. The Commander in Chief shared his fellow Virginians' distaste for New Yorkers, but if he was aloof, he wasn't discourteous. And, like the other colonials who had been sent to New York, his opinion improved as he began to realize that the city's reputation in the rest of the country wasn't entirely based on fact. He did, however, strongly disapprove of public drunkenness and there was plenty of that in Manhattan. He suggested to the Committee of Safety that unnecessary taverns ought be closed. The problem was that nobody could agree which saloons were necessary and which were not. They finally decided not to license any new ones and considered the problem solved.

General Washington's wife, Martha, was in New York with him, and together they did what every visitor always does. They toured the stores. Martha paid cash, so there is no record of what she actually bought, but a wagonload of goods left that spring for the Washington Plantation at Mount Vernon. The General, meanwhile, charged his purchases to his employers in Philadelphia. The Continental Congress was billed for two custom-made tents, walnut camp tables and stools, and special cases to carry them from one battlefield to another.

Washington was still not completely sure that the next battlefield would be New York. He had assumed the main British force was headed for there when it left Boston. But, in fact, General Howe had taken a detour to Nova Scotia. By the time his fleet turned around and actually set sail for New York, Washington had been in the city long enough to know that its defenses were woefully inadequate. His troop strength was a good deal less than original estimates, too, and though reinforcements had been promised, the American Commander in Chief knew he was whistling in the dark when he advised the Continental Congress that he intended to give the British "a proper reception."

New York braced itself for the attack. Everyone assumed Manhattan would be the principal target. The city's official records had been moved up to White Plains, the prisons had been emptied and their inmates moved out of the line of fire, women and children had been evacuated. On the morning of July 2 the British warships were spotted heading toward the Narrows, apparently on their way to the Upper Bay. Then, suddenly they stopped. Their target was not Manhattan, but Staten Island.

Howe met almost no resistance there and, by the end of the day, his troops were spread out over the entire island. It was firmly in enemy hands by the time the Declaration of Independence was read in Manhattan, and all of its militia had been willingly drafted into the British Army. It made a perfect base of operation and a good place for Howe to wait for his expected reinforcements. The sight of all those red-coated soldiers drilling on the Staten Island hillsides put a damper on New York's celebration of the news that independence had been declared and that New York was no longer a province, but one of the thirteen United States. They ended the day with an act of

defiance, by dismantling a statue of England's King George III in Bowling Green. But the general mood in New York that night was sombre. War was at its doorstep.

No one had any idea what the British would do next. The best guess was that they would try to take New Jersey and march north to cut Manhattan off from New England. Howe let them stew about it for more than six weeks. Then he surprised everyone by moving his troops to Brooklyn. Washington ordered his men to follow them and, on August 27, the two armies met. It was a quick defeat for the encircled Americans, who retreated that foggy night back into Manhattan and headed for high ground north of the settlement. When they looked back over their shoulders the next morning, there were no redcoats following them. General Howe was obviously in no hurry. Three more weeks passed before his men crossed the East River. After a skirmish and another defeat at Harlem Heights, Washington retreated again to White Plains, with the British following at a leisurely pace. The leaves on the trees at White Plains were at the height of their fall color before the two armies met again, and once again the encounter turned into a British victory. As the Americans scrambled across the Hudson to safety, Howe went back to Manhattan and reclaimed

Many of the city's great mansions were burned by retreating patriots at the beginning of the war, but this one on Pearl Street survived to become the official home of the state's first Governor, George Clinton.

CHAPTER 3

When the British sailed away on November 25, 1783, General Washington and Governor Clinton marched in triumph down Pearl Street.

it for George III on November 16, more than four months after his ships first appeared in the harbor. His troops controlled the lower Hudson Valley, Manhattan, Staten Island, Long Island and Northern New Jersey. General Washington, meanwhile, was establishing a winter camp on the Delaware River in Pennsylvania.

The war had passed Manhattan by. For the next seven years it was a British camp with enemy soldiers outnumbering the civilians by about thirty to one. But the civilians, though mostly loyalists, managed to turn the situation to their advantage. Judge Thomas Jones, who considered himself among His Majesty's most obedient servants, was beside himself with indignation over the profiteering that took place. His own estimate was that "the blood-sucking harpies swallowed up no less than twenty millions sterling of the money raised by Great Britain for the support of the American war."

There were all kinds of ways to make money. The American Army had already cut most of the firewood, and the British were forced to requisition supplies

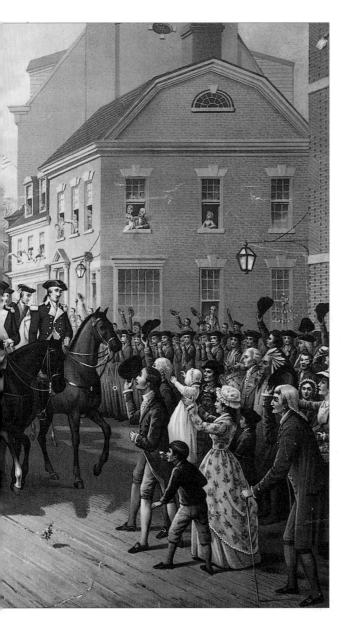

the soldiers.

According to Judge Jones, a carpenter who had appeared in his court before the war to declare bankruptcy had accumulated a fortune of £50,000 by the time the British left. The military authorities issued proclamation after proclamation to control what they considered rapacious prices charged by local merchants, craftsmen and farmers. But even threats of hanging didn't bring the cost of living down. High prices affected New Yorkers too, of course, but those with access to small boats regularly crossed the river to New Jersey to stock their larders. Others dealt with smugglers who brought them supplies by way of Staten Island. But the conquering British always paid full price, and then some, for the things they needed. When they tried to regulate prices, New Yorkers generally abided by the rules but added surcharges for transportation, for packaging, for anything they thought the traffic might be forced to bear.

Still, the English considered New York a wonderful place to spend the war. It was a lusty town where rum flowed freely, where the women were compliant and where an officer could take advantage of the same opportunities as local businessmen to turn a profit as buyers and resellers of supplies for His Majesty's Army and Navy. Theaters and concert halls were thriving, there was a racetrack on Long Island and, although the retreating rebel army had set fire to the city and destroyed about a quarter of the buildings, they took their rebellion with them to Westchester. The New Yorkers left behind were generally friendly.

But nothing lasts forever. When the war finally ended, some 15,000 former New Yorkers headed for Canada, but the rest were in the mood for a celebration. On November 25, 1783, General Washington arrived back in Manhattan and waited with his troops on the Bowery until they received a signal that the last British ship had cast off and the occupation had ended. The victorious army marched down Pearl Street, followed by the Commander in Chief and George Clinton, the first Governor of the new State of New York. That evening the Governor entertained the city's important citizens at Fraunces Tavern, during which no less than thirteen toasts were offered, including one to the Netherlands, another to the King of Sweden and the last in the hope that "the remembrance of this day be a lesson to princes." November 25 was celebrated as a holiday in New York for the next 130 years before all was finally forgiven.

from surrounding counties. Their policy was to cut wood from the estates of known rebels, which, to them, meant it was free for the taking. But woodcutters, cartmen and others in the chain of supply expected to be paid, and established special wartime rates. Before the war, the city had decreed that a cord of firewood consisted of four wagonloads. Under the new regime, the cartmen arbitrarily reduced it to three and quadrupled the price. The price of hay and cattle went up by the same proportion, as did the cost of housing

THE CLINTON DYNASTY

The first American Governor of New York, George Clinton, became Vice President of the United States in Thomas Jefferson's second Administration. He was a general during the Revolution, distinguishing himself, along with his younger brother James, also a general, in a battle against their uncle, Sir Henry Clinton, the son of a British Governor of New York also named George Clinton. James's son, De Witt Clinton, served two terms as Governor of New York, during which he spearheaded construction of the Erie Canal.

THE CENTER OF INFLUENCE

Among the people who drank to the health of the retiring General Washington in 1783 was a young artillery officer who had spent four years on the Commander in Chief's personal staff and had served with the Continental Army through major battles from Trenton to Yorktown. Five years later he would be instrumental in convincing Washington to come out of retirement to become the new country's first president. And, because of Alexander Hamilton, Washington's retirement would end where it began. In New York City.

As a delegate to the Continental Congress, Hamilton lobbied hard to establish New York as the capital of the United States. When Rhode Island neglected to send a delegate to the Congress, he raised the money to get them to Philadelphia, where they could vote on his side. Then he worked to get Vermont admitted to the Union so he could have their vote too. But his most important contribution was to provide Congress with an irresistible meeting place. They had, actually, already met in New York's City Hall and had been comfortable there, but Hamilton went to work to make it even better. He hired the French architect Pierre Charles L'Enfant to enlarge and completely remodel the place and, when work was finished, the building was quite the finest in America. The delegates who were invited to look it over were predictably impressed, and the die was cast.

Alexander Hamilton had strong political reasons for wanting the center of power established in New York. The American Government was brand-new, but he was at the heart of a movement to reform it. Congress had been routinely requisitioning funds from the various states, but was never able to collect the money. The result was that every state had a huge debt and everybody hated the creditor: the government they had fought so hard to establish. Following the lead of Philadelphia's Robert Morris, Hamilton became a champion of the cause to give more powers to central government. He also wanted a financial structure based on industry rather than agriculture. He had some influential enemies, including the long-time Governor of New York, George Clinton, who represented what New Yorkers still call "upstate interests," in favor of farmers over merchants. When New York was slow to ratify the new Federal Constitution, drafted largely by Hamilton and James Madison to reflect their Federalist views, the Assembly finally cast the deciding vote for adoption after a day-long demonstration in New York

City that ended with a banquet for some six thousand people. Among the suggestions made by after-dinner speakers was one that New York City should declare itself independent of the state and change its name to Hamiltoniana. The suggested name notwithstanding, as the new national capital, the city could easily have seceded from the state, but the old distrust other Americans still felt for New Yorkers made its new status uneasy. Even before Congress moved into its new quarters at the corner of Broad and Wall streets, Thomas Jefferson and other Southerners had let it be known that they wanted the capital closer to their plantations. Hamilton finally compromised with them, but only in return for their support for his financial ideas. The Federal Government moved out in less than a year. But if New York City wasn't to be the center of power in the new republic, thanks to Hamilton's compromise it was well on its way to becoming what it had wanted to be in the first place: the business center of a thriving country.

Meanwhile, New Yorkers made the most of their short-lived status as the meeting place of the first Government of the United States. When George Washington was unanimously elected by Congress to become President, he set out for New York with, as he put it, "feelings not unlike those of a culprit going to the place of execution." But the people who turned out along the way changed his mind for him. At Philadelphia he marched through a mile-long canopy of tree branches and, when he reached the end, a small boy concealed among the leaves neatly dropped a laurel wreath onto his head. At Trenton, he passed under a grand triumphal arch supported by thirteen pillars, preceded by thirteen young girls scattering flowers in his path. He eventually crossed over to Staten Island, after having been met by a delegation of Congressmen, foreign ambassadors and other officials. Then it was New York's turn to show its affection, not only for Washington but for pageantry itself.

A special barge had been constructed to carry Washington across the harbor. It was rowed by thirteen master mariners dressed in white smocks and wearing red berets. As it cleared the Staten Island shore, it was joined by a flotilla that seemed to include every available boat in the harbor, each decorated, as was the presidential barge itself, with red, white and blue bunting. A large sloop, with a stage built on her deck, held a choir singing music written especially for the occasion, and other ships carried bands as well as

CHAPTER 4

Previous pages: "It is done!" ... With those words, a flag went up and New York City swelled with pride. America had a President.

When he left home to become President, George Washington said he felt like a man on his way to his place of execution. But by the time he landed at the foot of Manhattan, he knew he was truly first in the hearts of his countrymen.

cheering people. Warships fired salutes as the barge passed, and on-shore cannons answered them with a roar.

It took more than two hours for the barge to reach the foot of Pearl Street in Manhattan, where the future President was met by the citizens of New York. A carriage had been provided but, because of the size of the crowd, Washington was forced to walk up to the new Presidential Mansion on Cherry Street. Every block was carpeted and strewn with flowers, every house was decorated with flags and bunting and garlands of greenery. Banners were strung across the roadway, and several triumphal arches had been constructed. And that was just the welcome. The main event, the presidential inauguration, was still a week away.

For that occasion, a coach drawn by four white horses carried Washington back down Pearl Street to Broad Street, where he disembarked to walk between

rows of his former soldiers. The six-foot-tall Virginian planter, who had always cut an impressive figure wherever he went, was more dashing that day than anyone could remember. He was dressed in a brown American-made suit with white silk stockings and silver-buckled shoes, and he carried a silver-hilted sword at his side. When he arrived at the newly converted City Hall, he was met by New York State Chancellor Robert Livingston, not knowing that only minutes beforehand, the Bible he would use in the ceremony had been borrowed from a local Masonic lodge. It was the only detail that had been overlooked.

The crowd fell silent as George Washington put his hand on the Bible and swore to preserve, protect and defend the Constitution of the United States. Then, as the new President bent forward to kiss the book, Livingston said "it is done," and a flag was raised to the top of the building. With that signal, the crowd roared its approval, and the noise of harbor guns and church bells all but drowned them out. The noise continued as Washington went inside to deliver an address to a joint session of Congress, and got even louder as the first President came out a few minutes later to walk up Broadway to Saint Paul's Chapel.

No one who was in New York on April 30, 1789 ever forgot that day, and none of them thought their descendants would ever take it lightly either. But less than twenty-five years later, the building that was the center of the celebration, Federal Hall, was torn down and sold for scrap. In less than one hundred years, the Presidential Mansion at 3 Cherry Street was demolished to make way for the Brooklyn Bridge. No city in the history of the world has ever loved ceremony as much as New York, but it has never been New York's style to stand still for it.

Almost no one in the city had any illusions that it would be the permanent capital, but the excitement was contagious, and influential New Yorkers went to work to see what could be done. The plan that

The first Presidential inauguration was held on the balcony of New York's former City Hall. Less than twenty-five years later, the building was torn down.

emerged called for rebuilding Manhattan, from river to river, at a point near the foot of Broadway. It would become Federal territory and would contain public buildings, palaces, gardens and parks grander than any in the capitals of Europe, and made even more impressive by the harbor surrounding it. The plan proposed landscaping Governor's Island, making it a lush setting for the presidential mansion, and it also suggested that, as the country grew, the capital could grow with it through the magic of landfill. Construction was actually begun on the first building, which they called Government House, near the site of the old Dutch fort at Bowling Green. It was to provide space to accommodate the President and both houses of Congress, as well as providing apartments for visiting dignitaries.

Hamilton's compromise ended the dream, but it also gave lower Manhattan a new lease on life. As his ideas for financing the American dream became national policy, New York was where the action was. In 1790, when the government began issuing bonds to cover its debt, John Pintard, a leading New York businessman, went into a new business. He placed an advertisement in a local newspaper, stating that he was was establishing an office to deal in the funds of the United States. "The advantages of negotiating through the medium of an agent, no ways interested in purchases or sales on his own account is too evident to every person of discernment to need any comment," said the advertisement. Within a year, Pintard and his partner Leonard Bleecker were holding stock auctions in the Merchant's Coffee House, a popular meeting place for monied New Yorkers, at the corner of Wall and Water Streets, selling as much as $100,000 worth of securities in a single night and collecting an eighth of a percent commission for their trouble.

At the same time, Hamilton's brainchild, the Bank of The United States, authorized the Bank of New York, another Hamilton enterprise, to sell $60,000 worth of its stock and, in the first half hour, it had collected nearly half as much again. The country was going through its first boom of financial speculation, and it was at its most intense in New York. James Madison worried out loud that such public plunder would put the governing of the people into the wrong hands. His colleague, Thomas Jefferson, who was also worried, took comfort in the fact that there were practically no subscribers from Virginia or North Carolina. But the states were united, after all, and the game was open to all. The bank stock, at $25 a share, was attracting well-heeled investors, to be sure. But government bonds, some selling for a dollar or less,

The City Hall building on Wall Street, near Trinity Church, which had been altered to create a meeting place for the first Congress, saw not only Washington's inauguration, but the framing of the Bill of Rights.

55

CHAPTER 4

Alexander Hamilton was a prime mover in making New York the country's first capital. He was also at the heart of the compromise to move it elsewhere to insure that his ideas about financing the new country would become national policy ... and to make sure that New York would be the financial center of the New World.

were also doing a brisk business among ordinary people. Speculators manipulated the price, but that only made the game more exciting. One official report said that in New York, "mechanics are deserting their shops, shopkeepers are sending their goods to auction and not a few merchants are neglecting the regular and profitable commerce of the city." A participant in the game gushed, "my whole rout presented me with one continued scene of stock gambling. Agriculture, commerce and even the fair sex relinquished to make way for unremitted exertion in this favorite pursuit."

The day of reckoning came with a resounding crash in 1792. William Duer, a former official of the Treasury Department who had taken off on his own to manipulate stocks and gain control of the New York banks, wound up in jail for crimes that included granting usurious loans to "widows, orphans and butchers" at rates of up to four percent a month. Duer blamed his troubles on notes that had been signed for him by one of his partners, John Pintard, the same man who had publicly proclaimed two years earlier that he was "in no ways interested" in buying or selling securities for himself. Duer, who had been threatened with lynching by his creditors, announced from the safety of his prison cell that he was secure and pure in heart and ready to defy the world. Pintard, meanwhile, stating that "I cannot foresee any possible advantage

to being in a debtor's jail," headed for the relative safety of Newark, New Jersey. He was probably right to exile himself. Duer spent the last seven years of his life in a debtor's jail and, even if his self-styled pure heart was in the right place, his creditors were never completely satisfied.

The panic Duer and his cohorts had started affected just about every businessman in New York, and many in Boston and Philadelphia as well. It weakened credit, depressed the value of real estate and caused rioting in the streets. But less than three months after the bubble burst, a New York newspaper reported "the shock at the time was very severe, but short of continuance." New York was prosperous again. Alexander Hamilton wrote that the recent unpleasantness was proof that "there should be a line of separation between honest men and knaves, between respectable stockholders and mere unprincipled gamblers." New York Senator Rufus King added that it served "to deter our industrious citizens from meddling in future with the funds and teach them contentment in their proper vocations." The message to Americans was quite clear. New York had shown that it knew how to deal with knaves and gamblers, and industrious citizens would be well-advised to put their trust and their money in New York institutions. America took the advice to heart.

A KNIGHT OF THE COMB

At the end of the 18th century, men invited to important balls often slept in chairs for several nights to keep their hair from getting mussed. It was hard to get an appointment with the best hairdresser in town, John Richard Deborus Huggins, who held court in the Tontine Coffee House, where stockbrokers and Congressmen regularly gathered. He called himself "A Knight of The Comb," but he had an even better talent. He was a public relations man. His clientele included the most important men and women of the day, and while he had them in his hands, he whispered in their ears. What seemed

like harmless gossip was really a means of getting the right message to the right people on behalf of such illustrious clients as Alexander Hamilton. There were more than twenty newspapers in the city at the time, but a word from Huggins had more power than all the words all of them put together could possibly print. In 1801, Huggins branched out to the printed word and became one of New York's first ad men as well. Eventually he wrote a book, which he advertised as "Exposing the art of making a noise in the world without beating a drum or crying oysters, and showing how a mere Barber may become an Emperor."

Part of Alexander Hamilton's plan for New York included turning the New Jersey countryside across the Hudson into the country's industrial center. He was killed in a duel there before the first trees were replaced by smokestacks.

A STREET PEDDLER MAKES GOOD

When the British troops sailed away from New York in 1783, among the soldiers who deserted and stayed behind was a Hessian mercenary who had signed up in Frankfurt as a means of getting free passage to the New World. He set up shop as a butcher in the Fulton Market and prospered. His enthusiastic letters to his brothers back home inspired one of them to seek his fortune in New York, too. As soon as the boy turned twenty he set sail for America, bringing with him a packet of flutes, some clarinets and enough cash to open a music store.

He couldn't afford the passage to New York and went instead to Baltimore, where he was able to sell his musical instruments for enough cash to arrive in New York in style. His brother found him lodging with a baker who exchanged bed and board for his peddling bread in the streets. The arrangement lasted only a few weeks. John Jacob Astor found it demeaning to be classed as an idle youth and, besides, he found other opportunities in the streets of New York.

He still dreamed of a music store, but he saw Indians trading mink and otter skins for worthless trinkets and decided that if he knew more about furs, his future would be secure. Accordingly, he took a job with a furrier and learned all he could, but he never thought of the fur business as anything more than a sideline until the day he met William Backhouse, the most successful fur merchant in America. Backhouse treated Astor like a son and, though he agreed that the music business was a good career choice, he convinced the young immigrant that the time was at hand for an American businessman to break the Canadian fur monopoly and that he seemed to be just the man to do it. Astor had a consignment of musical instruments on the way from his brother's factory in London, but decided to use the time before his ship arrived to find out more about the fur business. He became a purchasing agent for his employer.

The assignment took him to Albany, where furs were traditionally sold, but he kept silent at the auctions, having decided he could buy for less if he went into the interior. Even as a young man, John Jacob Astor was never charming, but he was able to make an impression on the Indian trappers by playing a flute he had taken along and, during the summer of 1785, he accumulated two boatloads of furs literally for a song.

It was then he decided once and for all that William Backhouse had been right, and his next trip into the forest was as an independent businessman. Before he left, he married Sarah Todd, whose head for business was as good as his own. She also brought him working capital in the form of a $300 dowry, and her mother gave them a place to live. One of the two rooms they shared was turned into a music store, which Sarah tended as John Jacob spent most of the next three years tramping through the woods accumulating furs. Eventually he ranged into Canada, where he watched the agents of the North West Company trading thousands of pelts with less effort than he had experienced with hundreds. Their profits impressed him, too. He decided to buy furs from them and concentrate on developing his own markets without spending so much of his time camping out.

He also knew very well that the Canadians were taking furs from territory that had become part of the United States and it was only a matter of time before the American Government would turn them away in favor of its own citizens. When that happened, he planned to be the only game in town. Back home, Sarah was doing all she could to make sure that New York's most influential people became friends of the family. When John Jacob came back from his buying trips, she kept him busy making the rounds of dinner parties and other social functions where he could meet and talk with government officials, local merchants and others whom she thought would be helpful to his career. It wasn't as though he needed any help. After fifteen years in the fur business, he had already become America's first millionaire.

Astor was not what anyone would call a party animal. He hated to spend money and despised people who did. He looked like the simple German butcher his father had been and when he talked at all, it was with a thick, guttural accent. But John Jacob Astor didn't talk much. Mostly he listened. And he took advantage of the things he heard.

Among the rumors flying around New York in 1800 was one that a man named Napoleon seemed determined to become Emperor of all of Europe. To Astor, that was a sign that he ought to find a new market for his furs. He moved quickly and sent a

shipload of skins to China. He also shipped them ginseng, a plant that grew wild in the New York area and which, he had heard, was extremely valuable to the Chinese. He had heard correctly. The cargo netted him the highest profit he had ever seen, even before the ship's captain had filled her then-empty hold with silks and satins, chinaware and fancy tea – which swelled the profits of the voyage to dizzying heights.

John Jacob's brother Henry, the Fulton Market butcher, was doing rather well himself. Though still a long way from becoming a millionaire, he and his family were solidly comfortable and he had enough left over to invest in Manhattan real estate. The fur tycoon had other axes to grind, but his brother's enthusiasm interested him and, in 1803, strictly as a hobby, he began buying up farmland in the upper reaches of Manhattan. Some of the properties he bought were from the politicians and merchants whose acquaintance Sarah had cultivated, many of whom were down on their luck and needed to turn their property into cash. Astor had plenty of that and he very quickly discovered that helping friends in need could be a very profitable enterprise. The more needy the friend, the lower the cost. And New York was growing by leaps and bounds. It was a terrific hobby and, often in a matter of months, he was able to realize profits as high as three hundred percent on his charity. But it was only a hobby. John Jacob Astor had discovered China.

The same year in which he began dabbling in real estate, Astor built his first ship to carry furs to the Orient. It was called *The Beaver*, but he had since found another fur-bearing animal the Chinese were more eager to pay high prices for. A few years earlier, a British explorer, Captain James Cook, had landed in the American Pacific Northwest and discovered an abundance of sea otters there. Officially, the territory known as Oregon belonged to England, but Astor believed, along with other Americans, that it ought to be part of the United States. After all, the Chinese would pay up to $150 apiece for sea otter skins, and it seemed a shame to let Canadian trappers claim them

in the name of Great Britain. Astor began telling friends he was outraged on behalf of his adopted country.

He took his patriotic indignation to President Jefferson himself. He explained that the Canadians were exploiting American territory, not to mention mistreating the Indians, and it was time someone did something about it. After painting a picture of a country extending from sea to sea, with new states eager to join the Union, Astor had the President's undivided attention. Then he got to the point. He told Jefferson that a growing country needed to be protected against "irresponsible fly-by-night traders" and proposed that the best way was to give a fur monopoly to "a permanent organization." His own company was a perfect choice, he said, and he went on to unveil a plan to set up a chain of fur stations across the Great Divide to the mouth of the Columbia River, where the bounty would be loaded into China-bound ships. The ships would then sail back to New York from Canton loaded with tea and luxuries to enhance the good life of the American people, and then sail back to Oregon with trade goods for the Indians in order to start the process all over again. It was couched as a completely selfless proposal and the President thought nothing of the merchant's request to name the future port on the Columbia River "Astoria." He also thought nothing of giving Astor a coast-to-coast fur monopoly.

It was a big enterprise and not easily accomplished. The Indians were less inclined to support the scheme than Astor had predicted, and they massacred the party he sent around Cape Horn to establish Astoria. Another party, sent overland, arrived in 1812, about the same time as the United States declared war on England. Before long, a British frigate appeared in the river and Astor's partners were forced to surrender their furs at about a quarter of their value. Astor lost $120,000 in merchandise alone. He was not a man who liked to lose. When the war ended, he went to work to recover his investment and, by the 1820s, his American Fur Company was regularly producing annual profits of more than $500,000. The business didn't do much for the great man's reputation, though. His employees were generally considered to be scoundrels, and at least one official report estimated that they were making as much as $50,000 a year selling liquor to the Indians in Missouri alone.

Astor had never been sensitive to public opinion, but in 1832, when he was seventy years old, he shocked everyone by announcing that he was going out of the fur business. He explained that Europeans weren't wearing beaver hats any longer and the price of other furs had become depressed because former buyers thought they carried the germs of cholera. Astor-watchers in New York said the old man had simply given up on life. His wife, his brother and his daughter had all died within a few months of each other and he himself was suffering from what local doctors called a case of "bad nerves." But in spite of the gossip, John Jacob Astor had not lost his nerve. He was about to begin a new career as the landlord of New York.

He already owned more Manhattan land than any other individual, and now his scheme was to improve its value. He began by demolishing all the buildings, including his own mansion on the west side of Broadway, between Barclay and Vesey Streets, and replacing them with New York's first luxury hotel. No city in the world had an establishment that compared to the Astor House. It had three hundred rooms and no less than seventeen bathrooms on its six floors; each was the last word in luxury. Its restaurant, housed in an imposing rotunda above the best-stocked wine cellar in America, was the first choice of people who mattered. And its black walnut walls, carpeted floors and crystal chandeliers were a magnet for tourists, even those who couldn't afford the previously unheard-of tariff of $2 a night. But there were plenty of rich and famous people who could, and its guest register was signed by luminaries ranging from the Prince of Wales to Davy Crockett.

The hotel did a turn-away business from the day it opened. Even during the financial panic that gripped the city three years later, the Astor House was the one place men chose to keep up appearances. They were

losing their fortunes, but Mr Astor was enhancing his. The panic was good for him in other ways, too. Homeowners and storekeepers were forced to mortgage their properties to stay afloat, and Astor was always amenable to helping them out. His seven percent interest rate was unprecedented, but no one had ever accused John Jacob Astor of altruism. And no one was surprised at how ruthlessly he leaped to foreclosure whenever the interest wasn't paid.

Until then he had concentrated his investments on

John Jacob Astor, who first appeared on New York's piers peddling loaves of bread, eventually owned most of the ships that docked there.

CHAPTER 5

By the time he died in 1848, John Jacob Astor owned thousands of undeveloped Manhattan acres, which had been divided into hundreds of high-rent corner lots by this 1811 plan.

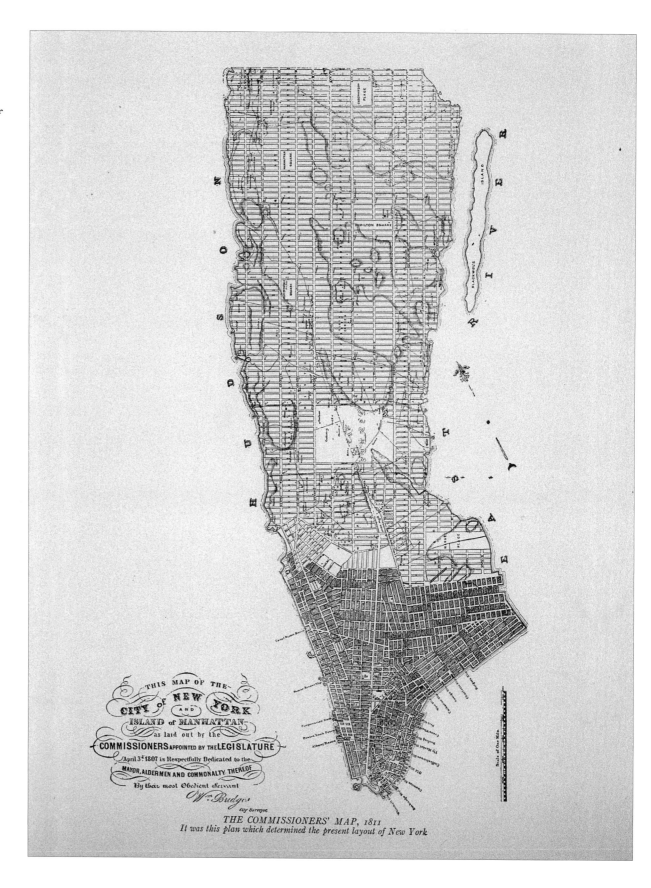

THE COMMISSIONERS' MAP, 1811
It was this plan which determined the present layout of New York

large tracts of farmland in the undeveloped parts of Manhattan, knowing that population pressures would eventually push their value upward. It was no secret. In the days when real estate was only a hobby with him, he explained, time and again, that the way to succeed was to buy in acres but sell in building lots. His 1837 foreclosures gave him an abundance of small lots with buildings on them and he discovered the profitability of renting rather than selling. It was a heady discovery. During the last five years of his life he earned more than $150,000 a year in rents alone. It prompted him to say that if he had his life to live over again, he would have owned every inch of Manhattan. Some New Yorkers thought he already did.

When Astor died, in 1848, an obituary writer said that his fortune was "as incomprehensible as infinity." His estate was valued at $20 million. He left $50,000 to establish a poor house in his old home town of Walldorf, Germany, and another $400,000 to endow a public library in New York. The rest was left to his family, chiefly his son, William Backhouse Astor, who shared his father's outlook on life. He took charge of the family real estate business and added some refinements of his own. By custom in New York, landowners had always granted fifty-year leases, but William Backhouse changed the term to twenty-one years. Tenants were required to build their own buildings on lots they rented and take care of the maintenance and taxes. At the end of the lease they had the option of removing the building within ten days or letting it become the property of the landlord. Very few leases were renewable. There was no need. The population of New York was growing faster than builders could keep up with it. Before he died, John Jacob Astor had predicted that his son would never make any money, but he said he was just as certain he'd never lose any either. He was only half right.

Even Charles Dickens could not have created a character like William Backhouse Astor. He was an ungainly man with small eyes and a big nose and a disposition most observers called sombre and mournful. His wife did what she could to keep up appearances and forced him to ensconce her in a Lafayette Place mansion that was the showplace of the city. They also had a house in the country and a staff of servants to see to all their needs. But William Backhouse's needs were simple. He loathed entertaining even more than his father had, and seemed happy only in front of the fire with a good book, preferably an account book. Occasionally she was able to drag him out to a party, but he finally put a stop to that by moving off to the country house. His life revolved around the Astor Estate Office, a two-room establishment staffed by himself, his son, John Jacob Astor III, and three clerks. The door to his office was always open, but he usually ignored anyone who came through it. He almost never looked up from his maps and ledgers, and when he did he never said anything. Most visitors found it prudent not to start a conversation either, and Many simply walked away after having decided to say what was on their mind in a letter. It wasn't very likely the letter would be answered, though. The Astor heir had long since decided that the best way to guarantee a profit was to cut costs, and he considered a secretary to be a needless expense.

In 1811, long before the elder Astor died, city planners had divided Manhattan into a grid-like pattern of streets and decreed that a standard building lot would be twenty-five feet wide and one hundred feet deep. There were eighteen lots in every acre, and Astor Estates owned thousands of acres. It was no wonder that the head of the third generation, John Jacob III, described his occupation as "gentleman." He could afford to. His holdings included rent-producing property on every avenue from river to river and, with a very few exceptions, on every street from 3rd to 186th, as well as on nearly fifty streets in lower Manhattan. It all produced an annual income of more than $50 million in the last part of the 19th century. But if John Jacob Astor III found time to live the life of a gentleman, making money was in his genes. He turned his attention to the creation of office buildings. And, as New York City began to grow upward, the rich got richer.

THE COMMODORE OF THE STATEN ISLAND FERRY

When visitors get to complaining about how expensive everything is in New York, the natives treat them to a ride on the Staten Island Ferry. Where else, they ask, can you spend a hour on a boat looking at the most spectacular man-made vistas on earth for a quarter? The proposition is even more impressive considering that in 1810, when a sixteen-year-old boy began providing the service, the round-trip fare between Staten Island and Manhattan was thirty-six cents.

The boy was a third-generation Staten Islander named Cornelius Vanderbilt, who cleared and plowed an eight-acre field to earn a $100 loan from his mother and used the money to buy a flat-bottomed sailboat. After a year of hauling passengers and freight across the harbor, he paid back the money and added another $900 in interest. To say he earned every penny would be an understatement. When the wind was poor, the sailboat had to be rowed. The days were long, but young Vanderbilt worked evenings, too. When the business day ended, he regularly shuttled Staten Islanders over to Manhattan for nights at the theater or gathering gossip in the local taverns.

But his little boat could carry only twenty passengers and the two-hour crossing made huge profits impossible. Cornelius Vanderbilt was eager for huge profits. Even before the end of his first summer on the bay, he began soliciting freight business from the Jersey shore and up the Hudson. Within a year or two, he became the proud owner of the biggest boat in the business. He also owned shares in two other boats and, though still a teenager, he was the most successful freight hauler in New York waters.

Most of the local boatmen, as well as the major shippers, were effectively put out of business when America declared war on Great Britain in 1812 and the British Navy responded by blockading New York Harbor. It wasn't much of a blockade. A single frigate stood outside the Narrows, waiting to pick off any merchantman daring enough to sail in or out, and another was posted at the western end of Long Island Sound. But it was enough to panic New York. The city came to a standstill. They were terrified that there would be a repeat of the British attack in '76, and their fears were finally confirmed when a fleet of English warships sailed up the Lower Bay. A heavy gale forced them to turn around, but no one in Manhattan knew that, and panicked New Yorkers were running for their lives. When the commander of Fort Richmond knew the danger had passed, he ordered his officers to take the message to Manhattan and called for the best boatman on Staten Island to get them there through the storm. It was no contest. Young Vanderbilt was elected. The men he delivered across the bay were seasick but still alive when they reached the foot of Manhattan, and Vanderbilt was the hero of the day.

But he had no dreams of becoming a war hero. Not while there was money to be made. When the war broke out, a military draft was instituted, but young men in other government service were exempted. A call for bids to provision the ring of forts around New York harbor seemed like a perfect way to avoid the

draft, and every young boatman for miles around applied for the job, cutting their rates to the bone. Vanderbilt was among them, but he built a handsome profit into his bid and became the highest-priced of all. He got the job anyway because the general who awarded the contract hated draft dodgers more than he hated profiteers. Vanderbilt chose to fulfill his contract at night so his daytime business could continue, and the shortage of boats made his business thrive.

When the fighting was over, he had saved enough to buy a dilapidated war surplus boat, which he sailed to Virginia for a load of oysters. The single trip, which gave a permanent aroma to the vessel, rendering it useless for anything else, produced enough profit to build a brand-new coastal schooner. Vanderbilt ran it with his brother-in-law, John DeForest, up and down the Atlantic coast in search of other profitable cargoes. His brother, meanwhile, kept the Staten Island ferry running for him. Three years later, at the age of twenty-four, Cornelius Vanderbilt had accumulated a fortune of $9,000.

But his real fortune was tied to an event that took

In the earliest views of New Amsterdam, rowing a boat from Staten Island to Manhattan was all in a day's work. Cornelius Vanderbilt often rowed the distance, until he found a better way.

Vanderbilt turned a tidy profit offering deluxe accommodations on his steamboats. But passengers who couldn't pay the price had to make do in rather more primitive conditions below decks. But from the day Robert Fulton brought steam power to New York harbor (facing page), the fire-breathing boats added new glamour to a trip up the Hudson or to New England.

place on the Hudson River on August 17, 1807. That morning a crowd gathered at the Cortland Street pier to see "a monster moving on the waters, defying the wind and the tide and breathing flames and smoke." It was the North River Steamboat of Clermont making her maiden voyage to Albany, with inventor Robert Fulton on the bridge. The 130-foot vessel, propelled by paddlewheels on each side and fitted with sails against an unforeseen change of plan, arrived at Albany two days later, after thirty-two hours of actual travel. The trip included a long layover at her home port of Clermont, near Saugerties, the country estate of Robert Livingston, who had put up the money to build the North River Steamboat.

Once having proven it could be done, Fulton and Livingston established a regular service from New York to Albany, with four stops along the way, at a cost of $7 a ticket. Livingston was Chancellor of the State of New York and he used his political clout to secure an exclusive franchise to operate steamboats in New York waters. He and Fulton could grant licenses to other operators, and they were also given the right to impound any steamboat in New York Bay, Long Island Sound or the Hudson River whose owners hadn't paid them for the privilege. The governments of New Jersey and Connecticut didn't agree with the high-handed attitude of the New York Legislature and encouraged competitors within their waters. Nonetheless, the Fulton-Livingston monopoly kept most of them away from New York City and deep in the red.

Vanderbilt was just as happy to let them all fight it out among themselves. As more and more of his competitors went into the steamboat business, with or without the monopoly, he expanded his sailboat fleet. His boats could haul more freight and were more reliable too. Steamboats had a tendency to blow up or set fire to themselves with sparks from their smokestacks. Still, they were clearly the way of the future and in 1818 he decided it was time to join them.

He went to work for Thomas Gibbons, who operated a steam ferry between Elizabeth and New Brunswick, New Jersey. The pay was low, but the

package also included a home for his wife, Sophia, and their two daughters at a New Brunswick inn which Sophia would run. As captain of the ship, Vanderbilt was also entitled to half the profits of the bar on board, in addition to his $60 a month salary. Best of all, it was an opportunity to learn how to operate a steamboat. But there was a catch. The new vessel Gibbons had built was a direct copy of Fulton's patented steamboat. Worse, Gibbons was planning to use it to expand his service to include a stop in Manhattan, even though he didn't have a license.

But under New York law, a ship couldn't be seized unless her captain was on board. Vanderbilt had a secret closet built in the hold of his boat and hid there whenever New York police came aboard to search for him. The game of cat and mouse went on for more than two months until one day when Vanderbilt got word they were going to board as he was docking. That day he put a little girl on the bridge, told her how to guide the vessel into the slip and went below with his fingers crossed. The police boarded before the lines were secure only to find a child where the captain should have been. They did find him a few weeks later but, before they could make an arrest, he told them that if they didn't get off his ship he'd cast off and take them to New Jersey, where they would be arrested. They did

As steam ferries (above) became more sophisticated, Vanderbilt began turning his attention to steam trains, and his public image, which he'd never cultivated anyway, began to take a nosedive.

as they were told.

On another trip, they managed to catch him on the pier and hustled him off to a waiting boat that took him to Albany to stand trial. On that occasion, though, he was able to prove that he had gone to New York that day on a busman's holiday. The ship was captained by a different man, who happened to have a license to operate in New York waters. The boat itself was operating under a Federal interstate shipping license. It was all perfectly legal. Through it all, Vanderbilt's reputation increased, and so did his employer's business. The man was so grateful, he offered to raise the captain's salary to $100 a week. The offer was refused. "I never cared for money," said Vanderbilt. He never mentioned his thriving fleet of coastal schooners, his boats in the harbor, his share of the bar profits or the income from the inn Sophia was running in New Brunswick.

Things began to change in 1824 when Thomas Gibbons challenged the Fulton-Livingston monopoly in the United States Supreme Court and won. It took some of the fun out of Vanderbilt's job, but he stayed on anyway. When his employer died, though, he refused an offer to take over the company. Instead he used the $30,000 he had accumulated to buy his own steamboat and went into competition with them.

But he was tired of New Jersey by then. After a few months, he sold out to his competitor and headed for the fertile shores of Manhattan. The man who said he never cared for money suddenly had a longing for more of it.

Vanderbilt established a steamboat service on the Hudson River, still considered to be the territory of Fulton and Livingston, in spite of the Supreme Court. He was such a creative competitor that it wasn't long before the cartel that thought it owned the river began paying him a monthly fee to operate elsewhere. He moved on to Long Island Sound.

It was a tough market, made tougher by the resentment of people in Westchester and Connecticut, who hated steamboats because they provided the means for New York City people to bring their wicked presence into their little communities. In the summer of 1832 their resentment knew no bounds. A cholera epidemic sent the entire population of Manhattan in search of relief in the country. It was a terrific boost for Vanderbilt's boats, but when they arrived at landings in places like Larchmont and Greenwich, they found

Before he completely gave up the life of a boatman, the Commodore, as Vanderbilt was known, established a transatlantic service with his luxurious ship, North Star.

71

In 1830, these fashionable houses on Bowling Green, known as "Steamship Row," were home to the great shipping magnates. Commodore Vanderbilt lived behind the fourth door from the left.

local citizens standing on the docks, armed with pitchforks and rifles. Vanderbilt responded by ordering that passengers should be landed on unsettled parts of the shore. He also began making longer runs, and by the end of the summer he had expanded his service all the way to Providence, Rhode Island.

Two years later, a railroad began operating between Providence and Boston, and its builders augmented the service with their own steamers between Providence and New York. Vanderbilt responded by putting the biggest, fastest, most luxurious boat on the Sound into service on the Providence run. Then, as he had often done before, he cut the fare in half by offering a round trip for the price of a one-way ticket. He made up the difference by raising the price of the food and drinks served on board. By the end of 1837, he had the largest fleet of steamboats anywhere in the world. Meanwhile, his Staten Island ferry operation had been taken over by his cousin, Oliver. But family ties didn't hold the Commodore back. He began a new line and cut the round trip fare, which had risen to fifty cents, in half.

By then his personal fortune had reached $500,000, and his career had barely begun.

In 1840, he acquired control of the Boston and Stonington Railroad, whose trains met his steamboats on the north side of Long Island Sound. He also invested heavily in the still-unbuilt Long Island Railroad and by the time it was open for business four years later, Vanderbilt's steamboats were carrying Long Island passengers and freight across the Sound from Greenport on the fastest route from New York to Boston.

But if he was interested in railroads, Cornelius Vanderbilt was still a boatman. When gold was discovered in California in 1849, as many as fifteen ships a day sailed from New York filled with fortune hunters. Many went as far as Panama, where they traveled overland to meet other ships to sail up the Pacific Coast. Vanderbilt decided to shorten their trip by building a canal across Nicaragua. He secured the blessings of the local government with promises of huge profits. The American government went along with the idea, and Wall Street had a field day speculating in the stock. The British government, claiming a protectorate over that part of Central America, eventually negotiated a piece of the action for England. Then the English bankers laughed Vanderbilt out of London when he told them his canal would cost $31 million. At that rate, pointed out a pencil pusher in the back room, every ship in the world passing through the canal at least once a year would produce only two-thirds of the revenue needed to make the investment profitable. The old Commodore wasn't too crestfallen. His agreement with the Nicaraguans allowed him to build a road instead of a canal, which he did. He was already earning $100,000 a month with his ships.

His price for the journey from New York to San Francisco was a third less than the competition and his new road made the trip the fastest by two full days. But he wasn't keeping his customers satisfied. In the rush to put more ships on the run, he manned them with less than professional captains and crews. When one

of them ran aground, the crew robbed the passengers, then took the lifeboats and left them to their own devices. The ships themselves were far beyond retirement age, and nobody ever characterized the trip to the goldfields in a Vanderbilt ship as a luxury cruise. Vanderbilt himself was careful to transfer ownership of the ships to the corporation he had formed, and was able to duck the personal responsibility. And when he began to feel the wrath of public opinion, he resigned from the corporation and began operating his own ships via Panama. When he tired of that game, he sold his ships for $1.3 million to the company he had abandoned and then signed on as their New York agent.

Commodore Vanderbilt was a private man who never flaunted his wealth. But in 1853, when a friend asked the fifty-nine-year-old steamboat king how much his estate was worth, he said: "I have $11 million. And it is better-invested than any other $11 million in the United States." At the time, he was dabbling in

Anybody who was anybody at all made it a point to be seen on the decks and in the saloons of the paddlewheelers run by the Fulton/Livingston monopoly and men like Daniel Drew, who beat the Association at its own game.

CHAPTER 6

transatlantic steamship services, and it was assumed that the twenty-five percent return he said he was getting on his investment was the result of casting his bread upon the waters. But instead he was quietly investing in railroads.

When the Civil War broke out, some of his ships were chartered by the Federal Government. It was a profitable enterprise, with individual vessels bringing him fees of as much as $2,500 a day. But he also lost several of them to the efficient Confederate Navy, and at least one was captured and held for a ransom of a quarter million dollars. It made him angry enough to offer his entire fleet to the Union cause, which left him little to do but count his money. Vanderbilt did better than that. He used it to diversify. He began by buying stock in the New York and Harlem Railroad, which ran up Fourth Avenue in Manhattan, from Prince Street to Harlem. Other investors laughed at him. The line never paid dividends and the city had passed a law prohibiting steam locomotives below 14th Street. But Cornelius Vanderbilt had an eye on the future. He knew the

Harlem line could be extended to the northern tip of Manhattan and, as he said, "If I don't get the benefit of it, my children will." He was sixty-eight years old at the time and standing on the threshold of a whole new career.

In 1863, members of the City Council circulated a rumor on Wall Street that they would soon give the Harlem a franchise to operate horsecars on Broadway, and the line's stock soared. The politicians' plan was to wait until it hit $75 a share, then they would kill the bill and buy the depressed stock for delivery at a huge profit, after having sold it short at the higher price. Before they could make their move, though, the stock hit 110. It looked like a bonanza in the making. On the day they killed the franchise, the stock's value plummeted thirty-eight points. Then, suddenly, their paper profit began to vanish before their eyes. Someone was buying up all the Harlem stock in sight. Slowly, the value crept back up to $150 a share. The short sellers had committed themselves to delivering the stock at $110. And to make matters worse, there were no more shares to be bought. Commodore Vanderbilt had them all and they were locked up in his safe. As long as they were there, the law of supply and demand kept the value rising. Finally, when they had to produce shares or face criminal charges, the councilmen had to deal with Vanderbilt, who bailed them out at $180 a share. *The New York Times* reported that "the shameless trick of the City Councilmen and their stock-jobbing conspirators has been paid off with compound interest. The lesson, it is to be hoped, will not be thrown away." There was, of course, another lesson *The Times* had overlooked: it was not a good idea to play games with Mr. Vanderbilt.

The manipulator of the Harlem scheme was another former steamboat operator turned speculator, Daniel Drew. As the biggest loser, he had the most to recover. In 1864, after Vanderbilt had also gained control of the Hudson River Railroad, the Commodore went to Albany to buy some votes in the State Legislature to allow him to combine the two lines. He had no sooner

boarded the steamer for home than Drew arrived on the scene and pointed out to the politicians that, while the bribes may have been generous, they could become fabulously rich by selling Harlem stock short. The lawmakers, who apparently didn't read *The New York Times*, stooped to the occasion and, on a signal from Drew, rejected the bill for consolidation. The stock dropped forty-eight points at the news. The schemers knew that Vanderbilt was short of cash and believed they had him where they wanted him. But the Commodore wasn't short of friends. Pooling his resources with broker John Tobin and speculator Leonard Jerome, Vanderbilt raised enough to buy every available share of Harlem stock. In their enthusiasm, they even bought 27,000 more shares than actually existed. The short sellers were committed to a price of $50. Vanderbilt and his partners had driven the price up to three times that much and Vanderbilt had the power to set any price he pleased. He had circulated a rumor that he was considering asking a

Vanderbilt's first venture in ground transportation was the Harlem Railroad, whose trains, often pulled by as many as a dozen horses in heavy weather, made one of their stops at the city prison known as "The Tombs."

Before he retired, Vanderbilt erected a monument to himself at Fourth Avenue and 42d Street, modestly calling it "Grand Central." It was neither central nor grand, and was rebuilt twice before this 1902 version emerged, only to be demolished a year later to make way for the new Grand Central Terminal, which has been living up to the name ever since. Turn-of-the-century Wall Street (facing page) grudgingly missed the Commodore. But there was plenty to keep them busy, and a lot more to come.

$1,000 per share when the lawmakers came to him with their hats in their hands. But after letting them swing in the wind for a few days, he established the price at $285, a cash drain of $235 for each and every share the short sellers were committed to deliver.

Vanderbilt, who made a paper profit of $25 million from the Legislature's shenanigans, quietly went to work to consolidate the Hudson and Harlem Railroads without the blessing of the lawmakers. Installing his son, William Henry, as the CEO of the Hudson, he began expanding its possibilities. He had his eye on the New York Central Railroad, which provided service between Buffalo and Albany and was the key to westward expansion via the Great Lakes. Vanderbilt's

line provided a natural link between the Hudson's railhead near Albany, and New York City. But, in spite of the fact that the Commodore was a major Central stockholder, the upstate railroad was transferring its freight and passengers for that part of the trip to steamboats.

In the 1860s, the Hudson River regularly became icebound toward the end of December, and steamboats were locked in port until the spring thaw. During those months, Vanderbilt's railroad kept the New York Central's city link operating. It did, that is, until the winter of '66. In January, when the river was solid, the Commodore ran a newspaper advertisement announcing that Central passengers using the Hudson

line between Albany and New York would be required to pay full fare. There would also be a surcharge for their baggage, and they would be required to get themselves across the river from Albany to Greenbush, the Hudson's northern terminal. Before the ice melted, Cornelius Vanderbilt had a year-round contract with the Central and had been elected its president. It gave him complete control of rail traffic between New York and the Great Lakes.

Vanderbilt was seventy-three years old by then and, if he couldn't down as many hookers of gin as he once had, he still enjoyed his fat black cigars, loved racing his horses and thrived on the company of beautiful women. Even before his wife died, housemaids at the Vanderbilt mansion on Washington Place spent as much time dodging the Commodore's advances as picking up after him. But when he became a bachelor, his sexual adventures kept New York's gossips titillated for years.

Among his other interests was the possibility of having conversations with the dead. There were dozens of self-styled mediums who encouraged him in this, but the most impressive of them were Victoria Woodhull and her younger sister, Tennessee Claflin. The thirty-year-old Victoria was described as "buxom," her twenty-two-year-old sister as "willowy." Vanderbilt chose the willowy one and invited her to take up residence in his mansion so she could be on hand if the spirits should move him in the middle of the night. It was a nice arrangement that made everybody happy, especially the housemaids, until the day the Commodore asked Tennessee to marry him. His children were outraged, but they knew their father didn't care any more for their opinion than he did for the opinions of any of the men he outfoxed on Wall Street.

The only possible solution was to find him a different woman, someone more respectable and – well – pliable. They found the perfect candidate in the person of Frank Crawford. In spite of the name, Frank was a twenty-nine-year-old Southern belle from Mobile, Alabama. She was a distant cousin of Vanderbilt's and, best of all, she resembled his late mother. When Frank arrived in New York, the old Commodore was instantly smitten. The following year, after setting up a lucrative Wall Street brokerage business for Tennessee Claflin and her sister, Vanderbilt asked Frank to marry him. To the delight of his heirs, he negotiated a pre-nuptial agreement giving her $500,000 in railroad bonds, and then packed her off to Canada for a quiet wedding. He was seventy-five, she was thirty. But this was no ordinary May-September marriage. The bridegroom was attracted to a woman who reminded him of his

mother.

The Commodore turned the job of running his enterprises over to his son, William Henry, and settled down for a life of connubial bliss. Nonetheless, he kept his hand in the business world and acquired the Michigan Central and Chicago's Lake Shore Railroad, which gave him control of shipping between New York and America's heartland. He used his railroad's rights of eminent domain to acquire a huge tract of land above 42nd Street for a fraction of its value and built the first Grand Central Terminal with $3 million of his own cash reserves. But he stopped there and turned his attention to making Frank happy.

Her needs were simple: a cousin in Nashville wanted to start a university, and the Commodore funded it; an Episcopalian minister who had accompanied her from Mobile was bought a church of his own in Manhattan; and, at Frank's urging, the Commodore established a seminary for women on Staten Island. Suddenly, Cornelius Vanderbilt was looking for all the world like a philanthropist. But his heart wasn't really in it. He had stopped speculating in Wall Street and began putting his house in order to make sure that the empire he built would live long after him. His days were clearly numbered, but he wasn't quite ready to go. He became severely ill in 1876, and the Associated Press sent his obituary to its subscriber newspapers. Reporters flocked to the house on Washington Place to see if the old man had truly gone to his reward, but were turned away by the Commodore shouting from his sickroom "it's a damned lie!" But it was a prophecy. The deathwatch lasted nearly ten months before Cornelius Vanderbilt finally gave up. There wasn't a doctor in the United States who would have bet a dime he could have lasted ten days after the first publication of his obituary.

The Commodore's estate was divided among his children, his widow and other family members. The bulk of it, an estimated $105 million, and control of the empire the old man had built, went to William Henry and his three sons. Though he adored women, the old man felt they had no place in the business world and left relative pittances to his eight daughters. It was "enough to let them live like ladies," he said. His son and namesake, whom he despised, was cut off with a $200,000 trust fund. Naturally, there was a lawsuit.

It was a nasty trial, with every scrap of Vanderbilt dirty linen displayed in the morning papers for the edification of the world. Then, after a few days, the suit was abruptly dropped. Presumably William Henry had made a settlement with the other heirs. But he kept firm control of his late father's business and, in the years ahead, proved that the Commodore's trust hadn't been misplaced.

His task was to manage the Vanderbilt empire, not build it, and so he had time left over to try to establish the family name in New York society. The old Commodore had always been shunned by the upper classes. He had been an uneducated steamboat captain, after all, and his vocabulary had been liberally salted with words not ordinarily heard in polite society. Worse, he had been a womanizer, a drinker and a cigar smoker. And worse still, he didn't care what anybody thought of him. William Henry didn't much care either, but his sons and their wives cared a great deal. They were representatives of new money, and to make them still more undesirable among people who mattered, the Vanderbilt heirs were still working every day on those noisy, sooty railroads.

The problem was the Astors. William B. Astor, Jr., the grandson of the old fur trapper, was married to the former Caroline Schermerhorn, who traced her ancestry back to one of the most successful merchants of the Dutch colonial era. She had strong ideas on how society should be structured, and pointedly snubbed adventurers like Cornelius Vanderbilt, even though his family tree included Dutch colonial farmers, a fact she overlooked when she decreed that the only people who really mattered were descendants of what she termed "the Faubourg-St. Germain group." Money counted, of course, but it was important to spend it in the right way. The city was awash with millionaires in the post-Civil War years, and Caroline Astor figured that somebody had to separate the wheat from the chaff. She appointed herself.

Among the Vanderbilt offspring stung by the Astor snubs, William Kissam, the second son of William Henry, felt the most abused. He had been educated in Europe, worked his way up in the family business as his grandfather had insisted and, when the Commodore died, Willie K. was a highly paid vice president of the New York Central. Better still, he had married the former Alva Smith, daughter of one of the most socially acceptable families in Mobile, Alabama. Alva dreamed

When Cornelius Vanderbilt died, the bulk of his estate went to his son, William Henry, and his sons. The old man had virtually ignored his eight daughters and cut off his other son and namesake with a pittance. In this fanciful representation, the keepers of the flame are (clockwise from top left) William Kissam Vanderbilt, the founding father, Cornelius, Cornelius II and William Henry.

Willie K. Vanderbilt pushed the family into high society after some creative pushing by his wife, Alva. Eventually, their daughter, Consuelo (right), made it into British society by becoming the Duchess of Marlborough.

of leading New York society, too, and she secured what should have been the proper credentials when her sister married the brother of the wife of the Duke of Manchester. It wasn't enough for Caroline Astor, though, so Willie and Alva decided a show of affluence was in order.

They hired Richard Morris Hunt to build them the most lavish mansion on Fifth Avenue and he succeeded admirably. Not to be outdone, William Henry commissioned Christian Herter to build him an even better house. He went a step further by assembling one of the city's most extensive art collections to decorate it. But he made the mistake of concentrating on American artists at a time when French painters and Old Masters were all the rage. "Taste will tell," sneered Mrs. Astor.

But what William Henry Vanderbilt lacked in taste, he made up in enthusiasm, and began following current trends by touring Europe in search of art and artifacts. Little by little, he lost interest in his business and, eventually, he decided to turn the day-to-day operation of the railroads over to two of his sons, Cornelius II and Willie K.

Almost no family has ever produced two such different brothers. Cornelius II found religion and became a pillar of the Episcopal Church. Most of his

Willie K. Vanderbilt's father, William Henry, gave New York its first Madison Square Garden, originally a railroad barn adapted for staging horse shows. He is seen here in the company of friends, watching proceedings at a six-day pedestrian contest.

money went to supporting the church's activities and most of his spare time was spent in pious pursuits. Willie K. on the other hand, was a social lion, a polo player, a party giver and a member of every important private club in town. But they both paid close attention to business and, when their father died, the family fortune had doubled in the years since the old Commodore was laid to rest. More than $200 million was divided among the new generation of Vanderbilts.

But in spite of their fortune, Mrs. Astor still refused to invite the Vanderbilts to any of her parties. Alva Vanderbilt was well known for her own lavish parties, and though all the best people not named Astor regularly called at the Vanderbilt chateau on Fifth Avenue, Alva was not the queen of society she wanted to be. But where there is a will there is a way, and Alva Murray Smith Vanderbilt was a very strong-willed woman.

She went about making plans for a lavish costume ball and announced that the grand entertainment would be quadrilles performed by the guests themselves. In addition to arranging for lavish costumes, groups of young women banded together to practice intricate steps and formations that would make them look better than all the other groups. One of the smartest of the cotillion sets was organized by Caroline Astor's daughter, Carrie. They had special dresses made and let the press know that they would outdo any competition as the Star Quadrille. Queen Caroline also had a special dress made for the occasion, but as she was getting ready for her final fitting, she realized something terrible had happened. She hadn't been invited to the party, and neither had Carrie.

Caroline sent a message to Alva suggesting that some mistake must surely have been made. "Why, no," said Alva, "I don't know anyone named Astor." When she pointed out that Mrs. Astor had never left a calling card at her house, the self-appointed doyen of society immediately had one delivered. "Oh, that Mrs. Astor," exclaimed Alva, and young Carrie, her mother and her father were invited to the party, which was later described as the most elegant since the days of Louis XVI.

Ten months later, Alva and Willie K. Vanderbilt were invited to Mrs. Astor's annual ball, whose exclusive guest list was limited by the dimensions of her ballroom to four hundred people. Mrs. Astor was still very much in charge of New York society, but on the second Monday in January 1884, the Vanderbilts had finally become part of it. It was not for nothing that when Willie K. built the largest private yacht in the world, he thoughtfully christened her *Alva*.

Cornelius II gave the family unexpected respectability by devoting his after-hours energies to supporting charities. His nieces, sharing this moment with him, and other third-generation Vanderbilts, eventually claimed a fortune twice as big as their grandfather's inheritance.

"And no income tax!"

It is almost an article of faith that the men who built early fortunes in New York had the good fortune of not having to pay any income tax. During the Civil War, however, their incomes were taxed, and heavily. But then, as now, there were tax shelters, the most important of which was an exemption from ordinary income on money earned through investing in railroads. It helped the country expand, and many a New York fortune expanded at the same time. Eventually the Supreme Court declared the tax unconstitutional. But when it was pointed out that ninety percent of any income taxes would come from New York anyway, state legislatures went to work quickly to override the Court's decision by providing the necessary two-thirds majority to amend the Constitution. It took them less than three years.

DOWN BY THE ERIE

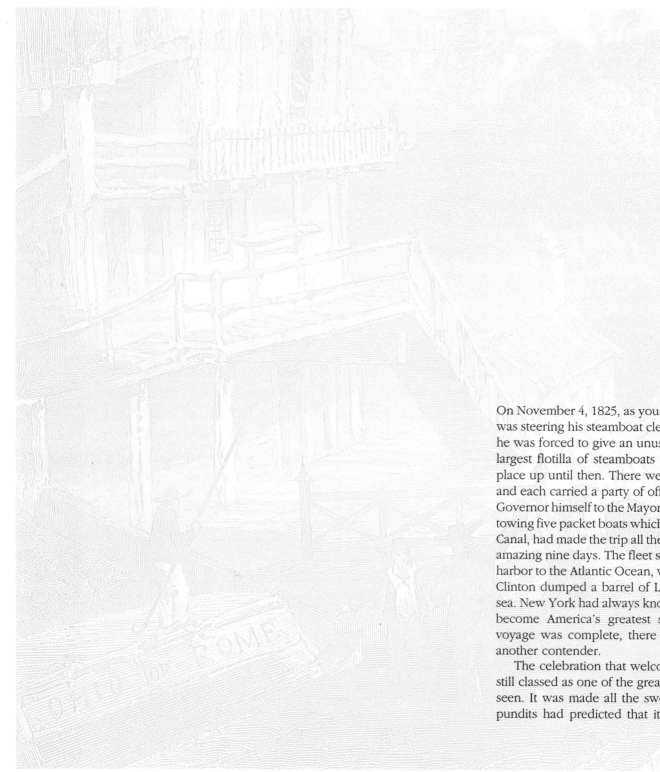

On November 4, 1825, as young Cornelius Vanderbilt was steering his steamboat clear of official New York, he was forced to give an unusually wide berth to the largest flotilla of steamboats ever assembled in one place up until then. There were twenty-two of them, and each carried a party of officials, ranging from the Governor himself to the Mayor of Lockport. They were towing five packet boats which, thanks to the new Erie Canal, had made the trip all the way from Buffalo in an amazing nine days. The fleet sailed down through the harbor to the Atlantic Ocean, where Governor DeWitt Clinton dumped a barrel of Lake Erie water into the sea. New York had always known it would eventually become America's greatest seaport, but once this voyage was complete, there would never again be another contender.

The celebration that welcomed the canal boats is still classed as one of the greatest New York has ever seen. It was made all the sweeter because so many pundits had predicted that it would never happen.

Much of New York's prosperity came down the river in simple barges and elegant steamboats.

President Jefferson himself said that the idea of digging a canal through 350 miles of wilderness was "little short of madness." It was, in a way. The job of moving trees and stumps, and digging a ditch four feet deep and forty feet-wide through solid rock as well as slippery bogs, all by hand, took as much imagination as brawn. But DeWitt Clinton had imagination to spare. His plan for the canal included eighty-three stone locks, a 750-foot aqueduct over the Genesee River and a sixty-acre man-made basin in Brooklyn to handle the barges.

At the beginning of the 19th century, produce from the Northwest Territories was shipped down the Mississippi River through New Orleans, which was French territory. Some of it also found its way to world markets through the Great Lakes and the St. Lawrence River, which was controlled by the British. The Louisiana Purchase eliminated the French from New Orleans in 1803, which made it a contender for the business New York so dearly wanted. But at the time, it cost as much to ship a ton of goods thirty miles overland to New York as to get it all the way to England.

The Federal Government refused to get involved, though Washington did concede that something needed to be done if the country were to grow. The job fell to the individual states, but none of them had either a good plan or the financial means. Clinton came up with the plan and, by the time he was elected Governor in 1817, he had already convinced the Legislature that the canal was good for the state and well-worth the $7.6 million it would cost. Before it was completely finished, eight years later, tolls on the early sections had already paid off the interest on the debt. And when tolls were eliminated fifty-seven years later, the State of New York had earned $78 million in fees.

By the middle of the 19th century, more shipping was passing through Albany and the Erie Canal than on the entire Mississippi River system. By the 1880s, an average of 150 boats a day used the canal and every one of them carried freight and passengers to or from

New York City. Just as importantly, the canal created boom towns across the spine of New York State. Rochester added 20,000 to its population and became the center of a new American wheat belt. Buffalo, which consisted of one house in 1814, had a population of 25,000 by 1839.

The canal also changed the way American shippers conducted their business. Before the canal boats began appearing in New York harbor, ocean-going ships never left the pier until their holds were filled with cargo. It was a convenient and profitable arrangement for shipowners, but it sometimes made the life of a merchant a chancy business. When cargoes began pouring in from the Great Lakes, Isaac Wright and Jeremiah Thompson, a pair of enterprising New Yorkers, began building sturdy, broad-beamed ships to move the merchandise the rest of the way to Europe. They boldly announced that the ships of their Black Ball Line would sail on the first of every month, whether they were filled or not. They were also able to promise delivery in Liverpool by the first day of the following month, and actually kept the promise by making the run in an average of twenty-one days. By the end of 1825, the Port of New York was handling more than a third of all of the export shipping in the world. Five hundred new businesses, including a

In the late 19th century, fashionable folks went to Long Branch, New Jersey to escape the summer heat. Excursion steamers took them to Sandy Hook, where they had to switch to a train. Contemporary illustrators came up with more colorful ideas for the journey. Those who stayed behind were treated to harbor views like this one on days when they could see through the smoke.

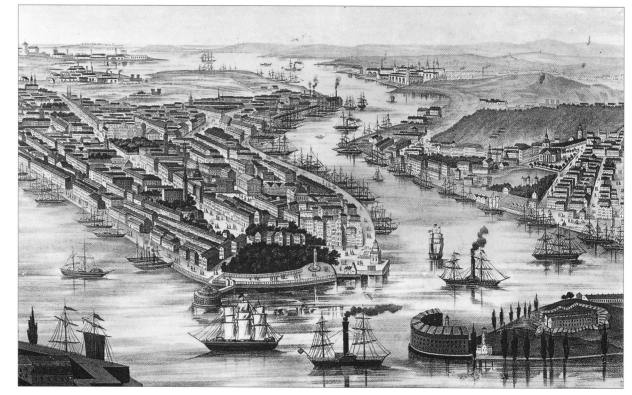

dozen banks and as many insurance companies, were established in less than six months. And, wonder of wonders, the New York Gas Light Company began turning night into day in the homes of those who could afford it. There were thousands who could, and they had the Erie Canal to thank for it.

But not everyone in New York State was rising up to bless DeWitt Clinton. "The devil take the great canal," wrote one of his disgruntled constituents. "It raises the price of land within a certain distance to double what it was before. Yes, and it lowers the price of land not within a certain distance in an equal proportion." Governor Clinton had anticipated such a reaction. In gathering support for the canal, he promised the people in what is known as the Southern Tier of upstate counties, that he would give them an east-west avenue of their own. He vaguely had a second canal in mind, but had since discovered that the mountainous country made that impractical. When the grumbling began, he ordered a survey to build them a toll road. But they had something more modern in mind.

In 1824, a year before the Erie Canal was opened, George Stephenson built the Liverpool and Manchester Railway in England. One railroad led to another and, by 1832, the Southern Tier of New York received authorization for its very own line, the New York and Erie. It would compete with the canal, but anyone with any foresight knew that canals would be obsolete in a few years anyway. The Legislature didn't have a lot of foresight, though, and it structured the bill to make building the railroad practically impossible. The charter authorized the company it formed to sell stock, but not to organize until half the stock had been subscribed. It also stipulated that the line should operate only within the borders of New York State and, to make sure it couldn't connect with an out-of-state railroad, it specified that the gauge of the Erie's tracks should be six feet, compared to the four feet eight-and-a-half inches that had become standard. The Legislature also neglected to appropriate money to survey the Erie's route, which made selling its stock impossible. When the officials of the new company went to Washington to find funding for the survey, President Jackson agreed, but overruled himself after an arm-twisting session with his colleague, the future President Martin Van Buren, a strong advocate of the old canal.

Wall Street was interested anyway. Once the stock finally went on the market, enough was sold in ten days to get the project rolling. The first president of the line, New York insurance magnate Eleazer Lord, insisted that the new railroad should begin on the Hudson River at Piermont. He had a summer house

there and apparently wanted to do something nice for his neighbors. The surveyors, who drew a line from there to the northwest toward Lake Erie, were forced by natural obstacles to dip into Pennsylvania at two points, requiring an alteration in the line's charter, and wound up at Dunkirk, a town smaller even than Piermont, on the lake shore. The route passed through Binghamton, a town with 20,000 inhabitants, but there were no other major settlements and not many people anywhere else along the way.

Construction had barely begun in 1835 when a disastrous fire destroyed a huge part of lower Manhattan and wiped out the businesses of many of the Erie's subscribers. Two years later, a financial panic eliminated more potential investors, but the Erie limped along with help from the state and support from people in the Southern Tier with visions of increased real estate values dancing in their heads. Five-and-a-half years after it was begun, the Erie extended all the way to Goshen. It was still a long way from the Great Lakes, but as far as New Yorkers were concerned, it needn't have gone any further.

Before the railroad, the fifty-mile trip from the center of Orange County to the center of New York City took two days. The territory around Goshen was already established as dairy country, but all of its milk

Before the 1860s, when the New York Stock Exchange was formed, broker-members of the Exchange Board that preceded it operated in secret. Those who weren't on the inside made their deals and their fortunes on the street itself.

Daniel Drew wasn't a man who liked parting with a dollar but, in what may be a classic example of giving until it hurts, he endowed the Drew Theological Seminary and Wesleyan University.

had to be converted to butter to prevent it from spoiling on the way to the city. Manhattan children were forced to drink milk produced by cows kept by local brewers, which were fed with the leftover mash that had been used to make beer. Suddenly the New York and Erie Railroad had a reason to exist. Not only could Manhattanites buy fresh rural milk for the first time, but the brewers were charging six cents a quart, and the upstate farmers made a nice profit at four. The railroad was making a profit, too. But it went bankrupt anyway.

The Erie went broke several more times before it was finally completed seventeen years after it was begun. The inaugural party lasted four days as a pair of trains wended their way across the mountains en route to Dunkirk. Before long, the line's western terminal was moved up the lake to Buffalo and its eastern end was shifted from Piermont to Suffern, where it could connect with a pair of New Jersey railroads to give it access to Jersey City, just across the river from Manhattan. Its profits were growing at a rate of nearly fifty percent a year, and investors were kicking themselves for not having recognized such a good thing years earlier. At the same time, the Erie was unusually attractive to small investors, who saw it as a perfect vehicle for taking a flyer in the market.

In 1835, a Wall Street fire wiped out 20 acres, 650 buildings and the fortunes of hundreds of New Yorkers.

Before the City organized a professional Fire Department in 1865, fires were fought by the so-called "laddies" of volunteer fire companies, who often fought each other as much as fires.

Then, in 1854, a Wall Street high roller accumulated enough Erie stock to get a seat on the railroad's board. It was Daniel Drew, the man who would plot against Cornelius Vanderbilt's Harlem line a decade later.

Like so many of the men who became millionaires in the 19th century, Daniel Drew could never be classed as a yuppie. He was just short of forty years old before he ventured into the world of Wall Street. But he was well-prepared when he did. In his early years he was a pitchman for a traveling circus that wintered near his home town in northern Westchester County. Later he became a cattle drover, a trade that taught him a little something about wheeling and dealing. Eventually he saved enough to buy the Bull's Head Tavern, a drover's hangout on the Boston Post Road, near the present-day 26th St. It was a long way from there to the bank and, as a tavern-keeper, Drew became the banker-in-residence for his former compatriots. It was then that he discovered there was more money to be made from money itself than from hard work.

But before he began investing in Wall Street, Drew put his money in steamboats, filling the vacuum left when Commodore Vanderbilt shifted his focus to Long Island Sound. Unlike Vanderbilt, he joined the Hudson River Association, the cartel that controlled traffic on the river, and became a member of its board. He himself owned two boats, but when he bought a third he placed it in competition with the cartel under a dummy ownership. At the next meeting of the Board of Directors, he announced that the new man had come to him with an offer to stop operating in return for a fee. They settled on an amount and authorized Drew to go pay the man off. He was back an hour later with the story that the offer hadn't been high enough. "But," said Drew, "I think he'll accept if you can come up with another $8,000." The deal was done. Drew pocketed the bribe and sold the boat to the cartel at a profit. Not long afterward he established his own brokerage office on Wall Street. He and the Street were ready for each other.

The man everyone called Uncle Daniel got religion as a young man when a horse he was riding was struck by lightning and killed. He took that as a sign that God

James Fisk, Jr. once promised that "I'll make my light shine like a bushel of firebugs." He kept the promise and then some. All New York knew he was a scoundrel, but they gave him a hero's funeral.

somehow seem more honest to ordinary citizens with a few dollars to invest. Once he had control of the Erie Railroad, he took advantage of them by manipulating the price of the railroad's stock. When the price was high he sold, and when it dropped he was more than willing to buy it back. In a single four-year period, the price of Erie stock ranged between $40 and $120 a share, bouncing up and down like a yo-yo, with no regard for the state of the market, or of the Erie for that matter. Every rise, every drop was carefully orchestrated by Daniel Drew. Everybody knew his game. He never made a secret of it. But no one could beat him at it.

Well, almost no one. When the Erie's Board of Directors was reorganized in 1867, Drew himself stayed on, but most of his manipulative cronies were replaced by men the *Herald* called "a batch of nobodies." Among them were two newcomers to the game, James Fisk, Jr. and Jay Gould.

Jim Fisk, the son of a Yankee peddler who had taken over and dramatically expanded the family business, was one of the most charming men who ever ventured into Wall Street. Women, especially, adored him, and men went out of their way to be in his company. When the Civil War broke out, he left New England for Washington to work his wiles on military procurement officers. He sold everything he had and when he sent back for more, he discovered that the war had cut off cotton supplies from the South. So Fisk went south and arranged to have cotton shipped north through enemy lines. When the war was over, he decided to get out of the dry goods business and began looking around for new opportunities. Wall Street was the only place to look.

It was where he found Jay Gould, who had visited New York in 1853 to see the exhibition at the Crystal Palace, the first of the great World's Fairs, and went home to his land-surveying job in upstate Delaware County convinced, after having seen at first-hand "what can be accomplished by means of riches," that he absolutely must become rich. He was back in New York a dozen years later.

It is hard to imagine two men so completely different as Jay Gould and Jim Fisk. Where Fisk was dashing, Gould was almost painfully shy. But, as unlikely a couple as they were, they were a team the like of which the financial world had never seen, before or since. Each of them lusted after money, Gould for its own sake and Fisk for the life style it could buy. Each was a financial genius in his own right, but together they were formidable, and the Erie Railroad seemed to have been created just for them.

had plans for him. If cheating widows and orphans was part of God's plan, He couldn't have picked a better man. However, Wall Street in those days was commonly considered to be a den of thieves, and a man who could move among them quoting scripture and out-conning the confidence men was, at least, something different. God's self-appointed agent also went out of his way to look different. In a time when men who arrived in New York to seek their fortunes made their first stop at Lord & Taylor or Brooks Brothers to dress for success, Uncle Daniel wore the same old patched and dirty clothes he had brought with him. In his later years, when his personal fortune was counted in the millions, he used an old umbrella handle for a cane. He was described as "narrow-shouldered, hollow-cheeked, tight-lipped and shifty-eyed." It was said that he never laughed, except at someone else's misfortune, and then only if he was the perpetrator of it. But his contemporaries also had to admit grudgingly that he had "the intellect of a fox."

His appearance, his religious fervor and his status among his fellow speculators made Daniel Drew

Their first victim was no less a person than Cornelius

Jay Gould's mother named him Jason, but though he changed it as a boy, even his mythological namesake didn't work as hard to find the golden fleece. Among his grand schemes, he tried to fleece the Government out of $100 million worth of gold.

JAY GOULD.

Making money and showing off were two of Jubilee Jim Fisk's great passions. When he bought a steamship, he appeared at her sailings in an admiral's uniform. But he outdid himself after bankrolling the Ninth Regiment of the State Militia. He had new uniforms made for his men and spent $5,000 on one for himself. The Herald said his waxed moustache looked "strong enough to run a soldier right through."

Vanderbilt. The Commodore had always managed to fight off the machinations of Daniel Drew, but when Uncle Daniel threw in his lot with Fisk and Gould, the rules of the game were changed. As the principal owner of the New York Central, Vanderbilt planned to protect his profits by colluding with the new Pennsylvania Railroad and the Erie to fix rates among them. The Pennsylvania's directors were more than willing and Vanderbilt thought he had the Erie in his hip pocket because he was not only a major stockholder, but he had a gentleman's agreement with Uncle Daniel. He should have known better. Drew may have been an upstanding Christian, but he was no gentleman. When the Erie board, led by Drew and his two new associates, voted down the scheme, Vanderbilt knew he had to come out fighting. He clearly had to buy up all the Erie stock available and use the power that would give him to drive the rascals out. But the rascals were one step ahead of him. Drew arranged to loan the cash-poor railroad more than $3 million in return for bonds under a contract that allowed him to convert it into stock and then back into bonds almost on a whim.

It gave him the means to flood or dry up the market and, in the process, keep anyone else from getting control. Vanderbilt's response was uncharacteristic. He hired a lawyer and took the Erie board to court.

When the judge ordered Drew's removal, Vanderbilt sent his agents into Wall Street to start buying Erie stock. But Drew had gotten there ahead of him and had flooded the market with a twenty percent increase in the supply. Meanwhile, he had also gone to an upstate New York court and not only gotten the earlier court order overturned, but, for good measure, had Vanderbilt's representative on the Erie board removed.

The New York City judge countered with an injunction against the issuance of any more Erie stock, but Drew had already printed the certificates. Jim Fisk came to the rescue by holding up the bank messenger assigned to deliver them and took off for parts unknown. Technically, since the stock had changed hands, Drew's hands were clean. The confusion continued for days, but Vanderbilt kept right on buying Erie stock as though nothing had happened. He accumulated 200,000 shares. But nobody had the

When Gould and Fisk engineered what became known as "Black Friday" on Wall Street in 1869, Fisk blamed the panic on the bears who "sold what they have not got." But the real problem was that the only sellers were the bullish Fisk and Gould, and Fisk, always the showman, made it appear they were buying.

CHAPTER 7

Almost a century before there was a game called Monopoly, men like Cornelius Vanderbilt and his cronies played the game with real money and real railroads.

stating that the railroad's business would henceforth be conducted from its depot across the river. Just to be on the safe side, they installed three cannons outside the door and hired a special force of local police to form an around-the-clock guard. Fisk became admiral of the company navy, which consisted of four fast boats manned by rifle-toting toughs.

It should have been Daniel Drew's finest hour, but he was like a fish out of water away from Wall Street. He began taking long, unexplained walks and slipping back to New York on Sundays, when Sabbath laws prevented his arrest. His partners, who had every reason for paranoia, responded by hiring a detective to follow him everywhere. Within a week or two, they formally removed him from the Erie board and circulated a rumor that he had been kidnapped. A series of legal maneuvers allowed all three finally to get back to New York, but in the process Drew had lost his influence with the Erie, leaving his pair of protégés with what they regarded as a license to steal. Gould managed to become the railroad's president and Fisk its controller. The Erie itself had lost $9 million in legal fees and bribes, but its new leaders had a printing press and they knew all kinds of ways to sell the stock certificates it could produce. It was true that stockholder approval was needed for the issuance of new stock, but Gould took care of that by rewriting the company's bylaws so that the only votes that counted were those made in person at stockholder meetings.

Once the legal details were out of the way, Gould and Fisk set out to make their fortunes. Their plan was more complex than anything Drew had come up with, and the old man was clearly impressed. He was so impressed, in fact, that he added $4 million of his own money to the pool they were gathering. Where he had manipulated the price of the stock of a single company, their scheme was to reduce the price of all stock sold on Wall Street. Part of the plan was to force up interest rates by cutting the money supply. Gould wrote checks on Erie Railroad deposits, had them certified to tie up the funds, and then took the checks to other banks as security on loans, the cash proceeds of which he stashed away in safe deposit boxes. In a few months, it was estimated that he had removed more than $30 million in cash from the New York supply.

As it became clear what they were doing, Drew panicked. He asked for his money back and when they refused, he began buying Erie stock short on his own account. His younger partners decided it was time they put the old man out of the way, and began releasing the cash they had hidden. Interest rates dropped and the market boomed. Gould, who had committed

slightest idea if it was a majority. All anyone knew for sure was that Daniel Drew and his cohorts had taken $7 million of Vanderbilt's money.

The Commodore wasn't the sort of man to take such a thing lying down. He raised a judge from his bed and secured an order for the arrest of the unholy three. When they got wind of it, Drew, Fisk and Gould loaded their cash and account books into carpet bags and headed for Jersey City, where they would be safe from the New York court order. The Erie's New York office was closed and an announcement was issued

70,000 shares of the Erie at $38 each, faced near ruin through the game he himself had perfected when the price rose to $57. But Uncle Daniel wasn't without ideas.

He went to financier August Belmont, who had lost considerably at the hands of Fisk and Gould and faced the prospect of losing still more through foreign clients of his brokerage business who had invested heavily in Erie stock. Drew agreed to sign an affidavit revealing what the rest of the Erie board had been up to and Belmont's lawyers took it to a judge who, in turn, agreed to appoint a receiver to run the railroad. But before he could sign the order, a different judge appointed Mr. Gould to act as the company's receiver. Gould was so grateful he named one of the line's locomotives for the judge. But before he did, he called in the press and announced that, as the receiver, he was questioning the legality of the stock that had been issued by the line's president. Few of the reporters noted that the president's name was Jay Gould.

Illegal or not, the small investors who had been holding the stock began selling it. Gould and Fisk bought all they could, using company funds, to keep it out of Drew's hands. But the old fox managed to buy enough to cover himself. He stayed out of jail, but the adventure cost him $1.3 million. It also dulled his enthusiasm for manipulation and he quietly walked away from Wall Street.

That was just fine with Jim Fisk and Jay Gould. They had learned all the old man could teach them and they had some good ideas of their own. Fisk branched out by buying a steamship company and regularly appeared on the docks wearing an admiral's uniform. His taste for things theatrical also led him to buy an elegant opera house on Eighth Avenue, the upper floors of which became the Erie's offices at an annual rent of $75,000 a year. Fisk's own office included a stage that held his desk and elevated him above anyone who might come to call.

But then Jubilee Jim Fisk was always on stage. His door was always open for reporters and he never failed to charm them. But when they said things he didn't like, he sued them. He had so many lawsuits pending, in fact, it was said he had a lawyer on retainer just to keep track of all the other lawyers. And though most New Yorkers knew that Jim was a scoundrel, they loved him for it.

Meanwhile, Jim's partner, Jay Gould, stayed in the shadows and quietly schemed to become the richest man America had ever seen. The scheme he came up with just might have worked. When it was all over, Fisk called it "a little innocent fun," and Gould tried to deny

Jim Fisk and Jay Gould played games in Wall Street that no one in the business world had ever imagined. But before they hit the street, they carefully made up their own rules.

In 1883, the Great East River Bridge connected the two cities of Brooklyn and New York, the harbor was bustling and the future was brighter than ever.

having had anything to do with it. But any attempt to corner the market in gold can hardly be called innocent, and that was exactly what became Jay Gould's consuming passion for more than six months in 1869.

The market in New York was controlled though a special commodities exchange set up for the conversion of currency into gold, the medium of exchange for foreign trade. It was all bought on margin, which made Gould feel confident that with the cash reserves of his railroad, he might buy all there was. There was a catch, but he was prepared to deal with it. The Federal Government had a huge supply of gold stored in New York and could easily stop any attempt to corner the market by releasing some of it. Gould decided to head off that possibility, but the key was in the hands of a perfect stranger, President Ulysses S. Grant.

They say that strangers are only friends you haven't met yet, and though Jay Gould didn't really have a talent for making friends, he made an exception in the case of Abel Corbin, a retired Wall Street speculator who happened to be the President's brother-in-law. He told Corbin that he was beginning to buy gold as

a means of helping Midwest farmers compete in world markets. If the price of gold was high, Gould explained, the farmers selling their wheat in Europe, and being paid for it in gold, would have more dollars. The country couldn't help benefiting, he said. He also pointed out that those same farmers would ship their produce on the Erie Railroad and that, he said, was why he was so interested. Gould added, in passing, that he didn't think it would be a good idea for the Government to muddy the waters by releasing any of its reserves, and, in return for keeping an eye on Washington for him, he offered Corbin $1.5 million in gold. Corbin accepted, but on the condition that the gift was given to his wife and not to him. Gould agreed. Mrs. Corbin was the President's sister, after all.

President Grant spent a lot of his time in New York, or at least passing through, and his headquarters in town was the Corbin mansion near Madison Square. Gould began appearing there as a frequent guest himself and whenever the President and his wife wanted to move on, Jim Fisk graciously provided them with deluxe steamboat accommodations or the use of his personal car on the Erie Railroad. As it happened, Grant didn't agree with Gould's economic theory and told him so. But the manipulator made it a point to be seen with Grant whenever it was possible. No one knew what they talked about, but everyone assumed Gould had succeeded in becoming a close financial adviser to the President. Smart New York businessmen decided it might be a good idea to listen to Gould themselves. They were sure of it when *The New York Times* printed an editorial supporting a free market for gold. They didn't know that Gould had paid a public relations man to write the piece and hoodwinked a *Times* editor into running it. Even after the editor was fired, few people made the connection.

Grant, meanwhile, was on vacation in the wilds of Pennsylvania and out of reach. Gould decided to move quickly before anyone started asking uncomfortable questions. He and his minions swooped down on the gold exchange and, before too many eyebrows were raised, they had contracts for almost $75 million in gold. To speed things up, Gould invited Fisk to wade in. The man's sense of theater was just the ticket and he was able to whip up gold-buying enthusiasm all over the city. As he did, the price rose. All the smart operators on Wall Street had previously bought gold short, on the theory that no one could possibly corner the market. Now that it began to look like someone could, they stood to lose huge fortunes, not to mention

their reputations. As they began putting pressure on the Government, Gould quietly began to sell. But Fisk kept up his noisy buying campaign and the price continued to inch upward.

On Friday, September 24, both men appeared in the gold exchange bright and early. Fisk made his usual entrance accompanied by fanfare, and his partner slipped into the background. The buying and selling was so intense no one could keep track of it. A mob that had gathered in the street outside prompted officials to call up a National Guard regiment to keep order. Then, just before noon, the panic suddenly ended. The Treasury Department finally released some of its reserves and the price began to drop. Mr. Gould and Mr. Fisk removed themselves to their opera house, where they hid in the huge safe, away from the wrath of the men they had ruined. Their lawyers were kept busy protecting them for the next seven years. And when it was all over, no one knew whether Gould and Fisk had made any money for their trouble. But no one could deny they had made history.

It made Fisk more famous than ever and, while his partner worked on the railroad, he became a successful theatrical entrepreneur. He also joined the State Militia and named himself a Colonel in the Ninth Regiment. It was only a ceremonial post, but few men loved ceremony as much as Jubilee Jim Fisk. He had elaborate uniforms made for himself and his men, and

In 1848, the view from the steeple of St. Paul's Chapel began to give clues as to what the future might have in store for the City of New York.

CHAPTER 7

bought his regiment the best military band in the country to accompany them on their marches up and down Eighth Avenue. He was still deeply involved in the affairs of the Erie Railroad, of course, but the energetic Colonel also found time for romance.

Not long after he arrived in New York, Fisk met a young woman who was quite the most beautiful thing he had ever seen in his life. She was tall, with long, jet-black hair and paper-white skin. One admirer, who said she had the figure of a duchess, described her eyes as being "like the phosphorescent streaks of light that follow a ship." Her name was Josie Mansfield. No one knew her occupation, but it was agreed that she probably didn't need one. Especially not after Jim Fisk came into her life.

Jim's wife, Lucy, who he said was "just a plump, wholesome, big-hearted woman," didn't like New York and, when Jim decided it was the only place to be, she chose to stay at home in Boston. He didn't seem to care and was pleased to note that she wasn't prone to surprise visits. It left him free to pursue other interests, but once he met Josie Mansfield, there didn't seem to be any other romantic interests in his life.

When he and Gould bought the Grand Opera House, Fisk bought a mansion around the corner on 23rd Street for Josie. Naturally, he moved in with her. Oddly, Josie wasn't completely pleased. She had never expressed any great feeling for Jim beyond gratitude for the luxuries he lavished on her, and when they became roommates, she began complaining that he wasn't giving her enough space to live her life as she pleased. What pleased her in the summer of 1870 were the affections of a young blade from Brooklyn, Edward S. Stokes.

Stokes was the operator of a family-owned oil refinery, whose principal investor was Jim Fisk. He called on Fisk at the 23rd Street house many times, and once he met Josie Mansfield, he became an almost permanent guest. Before long, Josie invited Jim to move out, and he did. He became single-minded about his business enterprises and his regiment after that, as if to blot out the memory. But the memory lingered on. His letters to his former paramour went unanswered, although she continued to cash his checks. Finally, Fisk had Stokes arrested for embezzlement, claiming he had stolen a quarter of a million dollars from the oil company. After an ignominious night in jail, Stokes filed a countersuit. The case dragged through the courts for months, providing newspaper readers with new reasons for getting up in the morning. Through it all, Josie made no secret of her true love by testifying against Jim, though most observers were sure she loved very little more than money itself.

The case took a bad turn when a grand jury found Stokes guilty on a blackmail charge Fisk had made against him and a warrant was issued for the young man's arrest. When Stokes heard the news, he began looking all over town for Jim. He found him in the lobby of the Grand Central Hotel on Broadway at 3rd Street. As Fisk was climbing the grand staircase, Stokes pulled out a gun and fired. Fisk died of the wound the following morning, his wife, Lucy, at his side. Stokes was in jail by then and Josie calmly told reporters that, considering what Fisk and Stokes had done to her reputation, she wished she had never been involved with either of them.

If Josie didn't love Jubilee Jim, New York did, and thousands turned out at the Grand Opera House, where the great man, dressed in his militia colonel's uniform, lay in state. Thousands more lined the route to Commodore Vanderbilt's Grand Central Terminal to watch as the funeral procession, led by the Ninth Regiment, delivered the Prince of the Erie to a waiting train that would take him home to New England.

Edward S. Stokes, who hired New York's best lawyers to defend him, went through three trials for the crime. The first resulted in a hung jury, the second in a sentence of death by hanging, and the third condemned him to four years in prison. He settled for that. Josie Mansfield left the country, and after a comparatively dull life, died in France, almost forgotten, at the age of eighty-three.

Jim Fisk had no sooner been laid to rest than Gould was forced from the Erie's board and asked to resign as its president. He didn't go willingly. It took a near pitched battle between railroad police and a delegation of U.S. marshals to dislodge him from his office in the opera house. Even before he was gone, the Erie's stock began to rise. The sharks smelled blood. Among them was old Daniel Drew. Armed with his own form of insider's information, he couldn't resist selling Erie short just one more time. Before the dust settled, Gould owed Uncle Daniel $800,000.

A contemporary cartoonist saw Wall Street as Jay Gould's private bowling alley. The diamond on his suspenders is probably a reference to his partner, Jim Fisk, who never appeared in any costume without his trademark, a five-carat diamond stickpin.

HONEST GRAFT

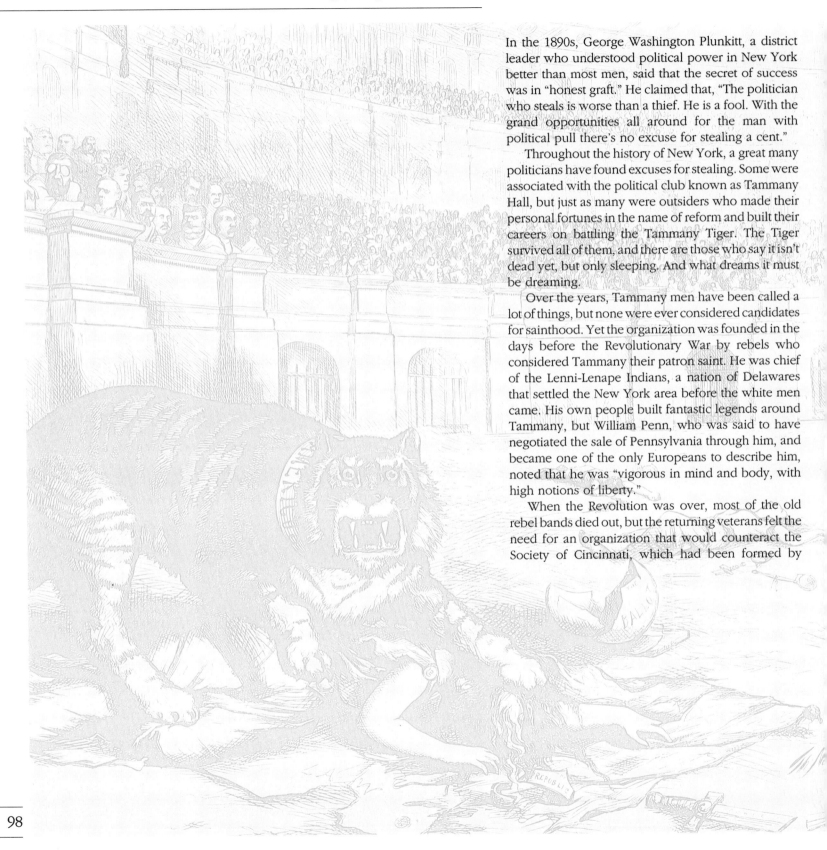

In the 1890s, George Washington Plunkitt, a district leader who understood political power in New York better than most men, said that the secret of success was in "honest graft." He claimed that, "The politician who steals is worse than a thief. He is a fool. With the grand opportunities all around for the man with political pull there's no excuse for stealing a cent."

Throughout the history of New York, a great many politicians have found excuses for stealing. Some were associated with the political club known as Tammany Hall, but just as many were outsiders who made their personal fortunes in the name of reform and built their careers on battling the Tammany Tiger. The Tiger survived all of them, and there are those who say it isn't dead yet, but only sleeping. And what dreams it must be dreaming.

Over the years, Tammany men have been called a lot of things, but none were ever considered candidates for sainthood. Yet the organization was founded in the days before the Revolutionary War by rebels who considered Tammany their patron saint. He was chief of the Lenni-Lenape Indians, a nation of Delawares that settled the New York area before the white men came. His own people built fantastic legends around Tammany, but William Penn, who was said to have negotiated the sale of Pennsylvania through him, and became one of the only Europeans to describe him, noted that he was "vigorous in mind and body, with high notions of liberty."

When the Revolution was over, most of the old rebel bands died out, but the returning veterans felt the need for an organization that would counteract the Society of Cincinnati, which had been formed by

Alexander Hamilton and others as a power base for former officers. The former foot soldiers turned to Saint Tammany. On May 12, 1789, William Mooney, an upholsterer rumored to have been a deserter from the Colonial Army, presided over the first meeting of the Society of St. Tammany, which he also called the Columbian Order as a means of attracting members who didn't fondly recall encounters with local Indians.

Tammany was a patriotic society, with secret handshakes and prescribed ritual, including an elaborate initiation ceremony, loosely based on Indian patterns. The New York chapter, known as the Eagle Tribe, was headquartered in the Great Number One Wigwam which, in its early days, was Brom Martling's Tavern on Nassau Street. It was headed by a Grand Sachem, Mooney himself, and thirteen other sachems, one for each of the new United States, each of whom represented neighborhood tribes. Other chapters were established in other states, but New York's was first among equals.

Annual membership was $1.25, and members were required to attend at least two meetings a year. Gatherings were held monthly for debating political issues, swapping anecdotes and singing patriotic songs. The meetings were livened by a clause in the bylaws that stated "the Brothers are hereby granted the privilege of calling for such refreshments from the Great Spring at their own expense as they may severally desire." They also turned out in full Indian regalia several times a year for torchlight parades and outdoor picnics that offended some New Yorkers but encouraged others to join up. But there was more to Tammany than drinking and singing. Each brave donated a dollar a year to a charity fund to help less fortunate members and their widows and orphans.

The Tammanyites gave up their Indian affectations after the War of 1812, when so many red men sided with the British. But in 1790, they were asked by the Great White Father, President Washington, to help him out with a problem he was having with the Creek Indians in Georgia and Florida. They didn't want to give up their land or sign any peace treaties, and the

Five years after its founding, Tammany had its own five-story wigwam on Frankfort Street.

Aaron Burr, the man who turned a patriotic society into America's first political machine, used Tammany Hall to insure the election of Thomas Jefferson as the third President, and his own to the Vice Presidency.

President suggested that after spending a few days in New York examining the glories of civilization, they might stop resisting. The Tammany Sachem responded by inviting the Creek chief, a half-breed named Alexander McGillivray, to spend a few days doing the town with the Tammany braves. When the Creeks arrived, they found an Indian village on the banks of the Hudson and they were overjoyed. After a few days of song-singing, sightseeing, theater-going and the consumption of much firewater, Chief McGillivray signed the treaty and the Creeks mended their ways. Thanks to Tammany, Florida was made safe for the arrival of thousands of New Yorkers a century and a quarter later.

This was Tammany's first venture into the political arena, and its success didn't go unnoticed. It caught the imagination of New York Senator, Aaron Burr, who had his eye on the presidency and saw the value of these men whom his opponent Hamilton dismissed as a mob. In 1791, he invited his friends Thomas Jefferson and James Madison to join him on a Hudson River expedition to study butterflies and flowers. They never got any further than Manhattan. By the time they left, Jefferson had offered Burr the vice-presidency in exchange for Tammany support in the 1796 election. The North-South alliance they formed was the birth of the Democratic Party. It also made Burr the first important leader of Tammany Hall, in spite of the fact he was a prominent member of the rival Society of Cincinnati and a wealthy patrician lawyer. But, first and foremost, Aaron Burr was a master politician. He never paraded in war paint, but he firmly controlled the Tammany sachems and, through them, he influenced the Tammany braves. Most of the propertyless rank and file didn't have the right to vote, but Burr knew they influenced small businessmen who did. Hamilton, who didn't have the common touch, said that Burr was misguided. "For the purpose of his ambition," he said, "Mr. Burr will use the worst portion of the community as a ladder to climb to power

The New York City Courthouse is usually called the Tweed Courthouse for Boss Tweed, the man who pocketed most of the money billed for its construction. It cost four times the price of London's Houses of Parliament, built at the same time.

Overleaf: Tammany's strength in the 1850s came from people like these who eked out their living on the streets. Top left: the Strawberry Girl; bottom left: the Radish Girl; top right: the Clam Seller; bottom right: the Scissor Grinder.

CHAPTER 8

and as an instrument to crush the better part."

Once having decided to take over Tammany Hall, Burr set out to make it a purely political entity. He used the society's braves to get out the vote, but he also used his influence to allow them to become property owners so they could vote themselves. Using party funds, he secured financing for Tammany members to become joint owners of parcels of land which, in turn, made them voting citizens. But it was a slow process. Hamilton's Federalists controlled the banks, which made financing difficult, and they also controlled the process for chartering new banks, which threatened to make it impossible. The least likely candidate for a new bank charter was Aaron Burr, but he decided to open one anyway.

In 1799, a yellow fever epidemic quickly prompted the State Legislature to approve Burr's request to establish a company that would bring cleaner water into Manhattan. Buried in the language of the bill, Burr had also secured the right to invest the company's excess capital in transactions consistent with state laws. He provided the water system, which in turn provided jobs for the Tammany faithful. But what the state had actually provided for Aaron Burr was a bank. The Manhattan Company, as it was called before it eventually became the Chase Manhattan Bank, began granting mortgages to anti-Federalists, and every one of them could be translated into a vote for the Democrats on election day. The people Hamilton had called "the worst portion of the community" were now able to vote against him, and they had the most powerful organization in American politics behind them.

Tammany's got out the vote for the Democrats in the 1800 election, giving them control of the State Legislature and the presidency to Thomas Jefferson. Jefferson acknowledged the importance of Tammany's support, but pointed out to the Tammany delegation which went to Washington for his inauguration that he didn't think it was important enough to dispense patronage among them. The Tammany leaders were stung, but it wasn't as though they hadn't discovered ways to extract tribute on the local level. It was a tradition that went back to its founder, William Mooney, who was fired from his job as superintendent of the city almshouse in 1809. His salary had been $1,000 a year plus $500 for expenses, but in that year he collected $4,000 in expenses and another $1,000 for supplies. When he was asked where the money had gone, he said he had spent it on "trifles for Mrs. Mooney." In 1837, Tammany Sachem Samuel Swartwout, who was also Collector of the Port of New

York, helped himself to $1,225,705.69 in customs duties and took up residence in England. The United States Attorney, William Price, also a Tammany man, went along with him, richer by $72,124.06.

If some Tammany men were self-serving, most were steadfastly dedicated to serving their country. The founding members loved America to a fault. Foreign-born men were considered for membership, but those who were accepted couldn't hold high offices. Braves were cautioned against buying anything not made in America by Americans, and the sachems were especially opposed to the new game of billiards, introduced from Europe, which they said had been brought across the ocean to corrupt American youth. They especially despised the English, the old enemy in the War for Independence, and again in 1812. But in spite of the fact that Irish immigrants were like-minded, Tammany hated the Irish even more.

Five years after Tammany built its own five-story headquarters building on Nassau at Frankfort Streets, a mob of Irish immigrants poured out of Dooley's Tavern and attacked the Wigwam. There was a message in the wreckage but, in 1815, Tammany wasn't quite ready to begin dealing with foreigners. The organization was more interested in expanding its base. The man who led them was Martin Van Buren, who gave them power in Albany, and eventually would give them a chance to try for what they considered to be their due from Washington.

Van Buren began his political career as a state senator from upstate Columbia County and, as a close ally of Aaron Burr, he inherited Burr's place in the Democratic Party as well as his influence in Tammany Hall. As an upstate politician, he was able to unite Tammany with Albany interests in the name of party harmony. In the process, he created a state-wide machine the like of which the United States had never seen before. But coalitions often mean compromise, and, in 1821, Tammany found itself supporting a new state constitution that would extend voting rights to citizens who didn't own property. The sachems, all of whom were property owners by then, and the braves under them, many of whom were also prosperous, weren't too pleased. But they also saw the handwriting on the wall. Waves of immigrants had begun arriving, and the Irish among them, especially, were natural-born politicians. Tammany knew that it couldn't lick them, so it decided to join them.

If Tammany didn't relish giving votes to foreigners, its upstate wing, Van Buren's Albany Regency, was also less than enthusiastic. The farm interests saw their power base threatened by thousands of landless city

103

One of the most interesting of all the Tammany Mayors was Fernando Wood, whose house on Broadway at 77th Street was a center of social activity, including a luncheon for the visiting Prince of Wales, the future Edward VII.

SUMMER RESIDENCE OF FERNANDO WOOD, MAYOR, 1855,_56,_57,_58.
Broadway and 77th Street, N.Y.

COPYRIGHT, 1913, H. C. BROWN.

Mayor Wood requests the pleasure of

Miss Mills _____ *company,*

on Friday, October 12th, at one o'clock,

to meet

His Royal Highness, the Prince of Wales,

at Luncheon.

R.S.V.P.   *Wood Lawn, Broadway.*

Please show this card at the gate.

people. But it was not for nothing that Andrew Jackson called Martin Van Buren "The Little Magician." He managed to overcome all the objections and maneuver the approval of universal suffrage by a two-to-one margin.

It marked the end of the Federalist Party and the beginning of a new era for Tammany Hall. The new voters gave Tammany complete control of the City Council and made Tammany man William Paulding the first elected Mayor of the City of New York. It also gave a seat in the U.S. Senate to Martin Van Buren, which eventually led to the vice presidency in the Jackson Administration, and finally to the presidency itself.

Tammany delivered New York to Jackson by a huge margin, and the grateful President lavished Federal patronage on the faithful braves. But when Van Buren followed Old Hickory into the White House, a devastating depression limited him to one term. It also shut off the flow of influence between Washington and Tammany Hall. But Tammany had other resources.

Thousands in New York were out of work during the panic of 1837, and Tammany charity was often the only thing that kept them alive. City employees who owed their jobs to the Society, routinely kicked back part of their pay to its charity fund. Tammany-appointed judges sold their influence to people who appeared before them, and donated the proceeds to the fund. At the height of the panic, Tammany district leaders were kept busy providing food and coal to the needy in their neighborhoods. Meanwhile, new immigrants kept arriving by the thousands, and Tammany men met them at the docks to steer them in the right direction. Those who followed the lead found easy naturalization through the Tammany judges, who were eager to make voters of them.

They carried the city for Van Buren in the 1840 election, but he lost in spite of them. On the other hand, they also delivered a powerful victory for the Tammany candidate for Congress, a young man few people had ever heard of named Fernando Wood.

Wood was a man with what latter-day political observers would call "charisma." He was also what would one day be described as "tall, dark and handsome." And he had a reputation as a man handy with a knife, a gun or his fists. His power base was a combination liquor, tobacco and grocery store near the North River piers, where he cultivated the respect and admiration of shipping magnates and stevedores alike. He tricked the Tammany sachems into nominating

him by recruiting his own followers to work in secret at the New York Democratic Convention, mentioning his name as often as possible and staging spontaneous demonstrations for him whenever the opportunity arose. By election day, the surprised sachems were happy to count Wood among their numbers, and by the end of his term he had charmed official Washington, too.

By the time he went back to New York, the Irish immigrants, whose numbers were still increasing, were well-organized into gangs, each of which relied on powerful politicians as their patrons. As a former Congressman, Fernando Wood became the patron of the toughest of them, the Dead Rabbits. The gang had been formed as an amalgam of several others dedicated to the destruction of the Bowery Boys, which led them into street fights that often lasted for days on end. Its legendary battles were often led by Hellcat Maggie, a veritable vixen who, they said, had filed her teeth to sharp points to make it easier to bite off the noses of

Among the ladies who appeared at the Prince of Wales's Ball in 1860 were the wives of John J. Astor and August Belmont and of George Templeton Strong, who wrote that the Hope of England "is a bore of the first order."

Nineteenth-century New York merchants looked down their noses at the antics of the Tammany braves in City Hall, and regularly voted Republican. But they knew in their hearts that the men who delivered the goods were in Tammany's hip pocket.

her opponents, and had artificial fingernails made of brass to make her scratching more effective. The boys at her side relied on hob-nail boots to stomp their victims, and used clubs and paving stones to make them otherwise uncomfortable. It was often necessary to call out the National Guard, occasionally with artillery, to break up their fracases. But their Tammany patrons controlled them more easily and used them in a variety of functions, from intimidating voters to restraining dissent at political meetings.

Fernando Wood used his power well. He won a four-way race in the mayoral election of 1854, and went to City Hall in spite of protests that led to riots. Then he proceeded to surprise everyone by becoming, as even his enemies had to admit, a model mayor. The day he took office he issued a proclamation against selling liquor on Sundays. More amazing, within two weeks, 2,300 saloons complied. He ordered pickpockets arrested and gambling houses and brothels shut down, and within a week the streets were dramatically cleaner. He consolidated city departments, claiming that they had been allowed to proliferate by the "greed of clubhouse politicians," and pushed through a law requiring banks to pay interest on deposits of its funds to the city itself, not to the Tammany men who had put it there. Moreover, after inviting the public to inform him personally of things they thought were wrong with the city, he followed up on their complaints, busying himself with everything from family disputes and holes in the streets to gouging hack drivers. Before he had been in office six months, he had set New York on the path toward establishing a city university and had steered away objections to creating an 840-acre park right in the center of the city. No one was at all surprised when Fernando Wood was reelected Mayor in 1856.

The boys down at City Hall nodded their heads in agreement at citizen complaints about crowded streets. But unless they could find a profit in it, they preferred to let gridlock take its own natural course.

That is when the real surprises began. In his second term, Mayor Wood began selling city posts to the highest bidder. Every job, from judgeship to street cleaner, had a price tag. The difference in 1856 was that the kickbacks didn't go to Tammany, but to Wood himself. Nothing was sacred. One of his cronies, who had obtained a judgement against the city in a land fraud case, demanded that City Hall itself, with all its furnishings, be sold at auction to satisfy his claim. It was bought for $50,000 by Daniel Tiemann, a future Mayor, who eventually sold it back to the city. The Mayor himself was active in real estate. He had a preference for corner lots and personally bought, at low prices, every one that fell into the city's hands.

It was easy for reformers to beat him in the 1856 election, but he claimed he lost because of the inactivity of Tammany, and bolted the organization to form a rival political club he called Mozart Hall. Amazingly, he was reelected again two years later. It was then he suggested that New York City should secede from the Union and become an independent city-state, "peaceably if we can, forcibly if we must." His request fell on the deaf ears both of officials and Tammany regulars and after the Southern states actually began seceding from the Union, he made a speech calling on New Yorkers to maintain the Union and stand by it "with our blood and with our treasure to avert the blow which a foul conspiracy has leveled against it." Mr. Wood was the kind of man who could argue any side of a controversy.

When the Civil War broke out, Tammany sent its own regiment to the front, and the braves back home

Every day of the week, the men of Tammany got new supporters by the boatload. The judges got rich making citizens of them, and the District Leaders welcomed them to their new neighborhoods, trading favors for votes.

went to work to end the career of Fernando Wood. They reorganized themselves and began a whispering campaign that Mayor Wood was unpatriotic. Very few of them were loyal to the Union themselves, but they had their regiment, which had fought in thirty-six battles, including Gettysburg, to keep that sentiment private. Wood knew he had been beaten and held out the white flag for compromise. He agreed to return power to Tammany if they would in turn agree to let him choose some of their candidates in the next election. The Mayor had already sold several promises for fees ranging from $100,000 to $200,000, and he himself wanted to go back to Congress.

He got what he wanted and served eight terms in Washington after that. When he died in 1881, leaving an estate of half a million dollars, one of his colleagues said: "No one here ever saw him put his feet on the desk or spit on the carpet." History was less kind to Fernando Wood's successor at the helm of Tammany Hall, a former fireman named William Marcy Tweed.

Among all the rogues of American political history, Tweed's name stands above the rest and he probably deserves it. But in some ways he was, as modern politicians often claim is their fate, a victim of the press. It is one thing to be a scoundrel, but quite another to be caught at it. However, even if he had never been caught, Mr. Tweed would have been remembered as the man who invented the political machine and became the first of a long line of big city bosses in every part of the country.

He didn't do it alone, of course, and his chief lieutenants were every bit as colorful as he was. Mayor Abraham Oakey Hall, known as "the Elegant Oakey," was Tweed's point man at City Hall. He never appeared

Many Tammany sachems, including Boss Tweed himself, developed their talents in volunteer fire brigades, and they had the time of their lives doing it.

anywhere, and he seemed to be everywhere, that the press didn't begin its report with a description of what he was wearing. He once showed up at a St. Patrick's Day parade wearing a green flytail coat with a green velvet collar. His shirt was embroidered with shamrocks and his silk tie, kid gloves and even his spats were also green. The frames of his eyeglasses were made from wood imported from Ireland, and were held in place with a green silk cord. No one took note of the fact that the Elegant Oakey's father was an English aristocrat.

He was a wiry, bearded little man who looked at the world through pince-nez glasses, could quote Shakespeare and the Bible from memory and regularly contributed articles and reviews to newspapers and magazines. He was a playwright, too, and frequently appeared as the star of his own plays. He was also a lecturer, in great demand at both communion breakfasts and stag dinners, and wherever he went he commanded the attention and admiration of everyone who listened.

He was an influential member of every important club in town, a respected member of society, and far from the stereotype of a Tammany politician. Even Tweed had to admit that Oakey was probably in over his head in the world of politics. But Oakey was clearly in politics for the fun of it, and very few of New York's mayors ever had such a good time at City Hall. Becoming Mayor was certainly not his lifelong ambition. Before joining Tammany, Oakey was a Republican. But as a lawyer representing robber barons and city officials, he realized that a new party label would be good for business. It was good for his career too, after Fernando Wood made him District Attorney, which placed him at the center of influence as the person who could easily neglect to prosecute selected cases. Among those overlooked were charges against at least 10,000 saloon keepers, all of them Irish, which made him so popular with them that he could have shown up at the St. Patrick's Day parade wearing an orange suit.

Another of Tweed's key henchmen was Peter Sweeny, better known as "Brains," who worked behind the scenes to keep the wheels of the machine turning. He had risen through the Tammany ranks, remembering every favor and every slight, and learning how to keep the braves in line. Like Oakey Hall, he had been District Attorney, but resigned quickly when he was overcome by stage fright during his first appearance before a jury. But though Brains Sweeny may have been tongue-tied in front of a group, he was considered to be one of the most effective lobbyists ever to work the corridors of the New York State Legislature, where he labored in behalf of the railroads and Tammany

Hall. He carefully shunned the role of leader and modestly claimed that he had nothing but "the public welfare and the prosperity of my friends at heart." He was a man after Boss Tweed's own heart.

Also at the heart of what was known as the Tweed Ring was Richard Connolly, affectionately known as "Slippery Dick." As a high Tammany sachem, and boss of the most important Irish ward in the city, he had risen to the post of City Comptroller. A biographer described him as "cold, crafty and cowardly with a smooth, oily manner." He was also said to have been a man without a single honest instinct, but without the courage to be a fraud. To which Tweed added, "we could not get along without him." It was an understatement. Slippery Dick had his hands on the city's purse strings, and Tweed had him in his hip pocket.

William Marcy Tweed was a natural-born politician, but he grew up on Manhattan's Lower East Side with the dream of becoming an accountant. He began combining his talent for manipulating numbers with his ability for influencing people when he joined the Americus Engine Company, the city's most famous volunteer fire department, and became its foreman in less than six months. The fire departments of the day controlled block votes for political candidates, making

Tammany's strength came from Lower East Side immigrants (facing page), from shop girls who rode horsecars to work (above), and even from kids who earned their keep selling newspapers (left).

In New York's Gilded Age, the rich went to Delmonico's for feasts of clams and oysters, but the poor weren't denied such pleasures as long as they could scrape together a few pennies.

them important to Tammany, which invited Tweed to preside over one of its meetings when he was still in his early twenties. It was a heady experience, and by the time he was thirty, Tweed, already a member of the Board of Aldermen, was a successful candidate for Congress. After two years in Washington, he decided that he could do better in New York and became a member of the City's Board of Education, where he could share the profits with companies selling textbooks, and collect fees from job-hunting teachers. He went from there to the Board of Supervisors, where a man could feed at the public trough without any danger of discovery because of the complexity of deals that

could be made in funding and regulating every department in the City Government. He very nearly made a lifetime career of the job, turning down several better ones, until the Board was disbanded in 1870. By then, Mr. Tweed had learned enough about graft to set up his own similar den of thieves, and he paved the way for it by blowing the whistle on his former colleagues. He had meanwhile managed to get himself elected to the State Senate and appointed to the job of Deputy Street Commissioner. He also had several million dollars in the bank.

According to a local legend in Albany, when Tweed arrived in the Senate, they had to provide a special chair for him. He weighed close to three hundred pounds, but he was more than fat. A six-footer, William Marcy Tweed was a big man in every sense of the word, from his head and shoulders to his hands and feet. His eyes twinkled as brightly as the diamond he flaunted from the front of his shirt and he seemed for all the world like an overgrown teddy bear. His political enemies followed the lead of Thomas Nast, the *Herald's* cartoonist, in characterizing Tweed as a tiger, which had been the symbol of the Americus Engine Company. But he had more friends than enemies, and that was the key to his success.

He gave up drinking when he went into politics and he never smoked, but he was as at home, and as welcome, in slum neighborhood saloons as in the most sophisticated uptown clubs. And he had genuine friends and admirers in both. He was almost as poor

at public speaking as his crony Brains Sweeny, but he inspired confidence in everyone he met face to face. And what inspired them most was his honesty. Though it seems like a contradiction, Tweed was, in fact, scrupulously honest. He never made a promise he couldn't keep and he kept every one he made. Unfortunately, he made too many promises to the wrong people. Nobody knows for sure how many millions of dollars left the city treasury to help him keep his promises of payoffs to contractors and suppliers. On the other hand, he also kept his word to thousands who sincerely needed his help and that was the real source of his power.

He was also a man for his times. The waves of immigrants who arrived in New York in the years just before the Civil War had changed the city dramatically, and the government that had functioned so well from

Alfresco dining, no matter how inexpensive, wasn't always possible in 19th-century New York. Most streets were routinely ignored by Tammany's Sanitation Commissioners.

Jim Fisk (right) became a Tammany fellow-traveler when he signed on Boss Tweed as a partner in his Erie Railroad manipulations. Meanwhile, most New Yorkers and their children were discovering that hard work isn't always the way to make a fortune.

Colonial times wasn't able to adjust to the new problems that growth had brought. The state government was still in the hands of farm interests, which had always distrusted the city and were beginning to run from it in panic. Albany looked down the river and saw what it considered to be an evil thing, a collection of poor, uneducated foreigners mixed with a population of latent criminals. In their view, the best way to handle the problem was to reduce the size of the government in hopes that someone else would provide an answer, preferably not with their tax money. They began to agree with Alexander Hamilton that the people are a beast best kept at arm's length, and the government should be in the hands of an élite educated class who really, after all, knew what was best.

But what had been best in Hamilton's time didn't work any longer. The business interests felt they needed special attention and so did the immigrants. Reformers were caught in the middle, and the only people who could work both sides of the street were

professional politicians who weren't above being bribed by businessmen and could get immigrant votes in return for jobs. The Civil War, meanwhile, had made most people cynical about what the world was coming to. They saw men who had passionately crusaded against slavery buy their way out of the draft when the time came for them to fight for their beliefs. And they had dodged brickbats and lynch mobs when the poor decided they didn't want to go either. They had seen men become overnight millionaires, and then watched as the new tycoons and the politicians made lucrative deals with each other. It was the same in every city and even in the Federal Government. It took a New Yorker

to bring order out of the chaos and take advantage of the apathy to create something brand-new in American politics.

Tweed claimed that he organized his ring after he became a State Senator. He said that it wasn't possible to get anything done in Albany without paying for it, and that his purpose was to raise funds for payoffs that would protect the city. But in the process he also increased his own power. Among the men on his under-the-table payroll was State Supreme Court Judge George Barnard, who was worth a considerable amount because, as Tweed pointed out, "it's better to know the judge than to know the law." It was Barnard who

The richest men in late 19th-century America gathered under a portrait of Commodore Vanderbilt, a man who was no stranger to hard work, but who showed them all it wasn't necessary.

Some New Yorkers (right) eked out a living collecting discarded rags. Out on Ellis Island, thousands of future New Yorkers (below right) wondered if that was what fate had in store for them, or whether they'd wind up on Park Avenue, where their meals would be cheerfully delivered (facing page).

helped Jim Fisk and Jay Gould run the Erie Railroad to their advantage, and it was Tweed who introduced them to him. Tweed also had two other judges on his payroll, whom he used to admit aspiring lawyers to the bar. They were also kept busy naturalizing new citizens so Tammany could have their votes.

If Tweed had decided to become a businessman rather than a politician, he'd probably have been the most successful of them all. In fact, he was a businessman and he was successful. One of his early enterprises was the New York Printing company, whose presses ground out all the forms the city bought. The stationery used by the City Council alone brought in $400,000 a year. Tweed's company also printed all the naturalization papers used in New York at the time and sold them for fifty cents apiece to hopeful immigrants. And it published a newspaper that ran all of the city's advertising and legal notices. Tweed was also on the Erie Railroad's Board of Directors and served as its chief lobbyist in the Albany Legislature, a sideline that made him almost as rich as the manipulators in charge.

Like the railroad barons, Tweed made no secret of his activities and, when challenged, he disdainfully said, "What are you going to do about it?" Nobody seemed inclined to do anything except watch as he flaunted his wealth. Always a devoted family man, he put on the greatest show of his life when his daughter, Mary Amelia, married Arthur Ambrose Maginnis in 1871. All of New York society turned up at Trinity Church to watch the great man give the bride away, and then went on to the Tweed mansion on Fifth Avenue at 43rd Street for a party which *The New York Sun* said "beggared description." Nonetheless, one reporter gave it a try. "Imagine," he wrote, "the utmost brilliancy and hundreds of ladies and gentlemen in all the gorgeousness of full dress and flashing with diamonds; listen to the delicious strains of the band and inhale, in spirit, the sweet perfume, and some inadequate notion can be formed of the magnificence of the scene." The gifts filled an entire room, and the *Tribune* reported that it was the greatest such collection since the wedding of the daughter of the Khedive of Egypt. It included no less than forty sets of silver and a necklace of diamonds which *The Times* said were "as big as filberts." Gifts of cash weren't on display, but it was estimated that they added up to $700,000. James Gordon Bennett of the *Tribune* said he wasn't impressed, but he ruminated editorially that the wedding was nothing less than a tribute to Democracy. "Come to its fountainhead, the old Wigwam," he wrote, "and there you get into a Democratic placer which gives you, without the labor of digging, the pearls of Ceylon,

Many of the immigrant children were kept off the streets thanks to settlement houses (above). The fathers of some of them took to the streets to sell flowers (right) to fancy ladies outside the Fifth Avenue Hotel, while their mothers often pitched in with street corner pretzel stands (facing page).

the gold of California and the diamonds of Golconda. And it all comes out of the tax levy." To which Tweed replied, one more time, "What are you going to do about it?".

In addition to lavishing riches and affection on his family, the Boss was also generous with charities. In 1870 alone, he donated $50,000 to the poor, and he encouraged the city itself to match it. He also saw to it that the city donated $1.3 million to the Catholic Church and, so no one would feel slighted, it divided another $300,000 among other religious organizations.

But good works notwithstanding, nearly every newspaper in town attacked Tweed nearly every day, but though the *Tribune* told its readers that the Tweed Ring was "the most corrupt gang of political adventurers that ever robbed a helpless city," and *The Times* said "though every Democrat is not a horse thief, every horse thief is a Democrat," they were just empty words without facts and figures to back them up. Citizens smiled at Thomas Nast's clever cartoons in *Harper's Weekly*, but no one seemed to be too concerned. Tweed responded to some of the attacks by buying the newspapers, which then went to work to attack the opposition press, many of whose reporters were also placed on the city payroll. *The World*, which was owned by the Tweed Ring, discredited *The Times* by pointing out that its editor was not only an Englishman, but married to an actress at that. It accused the *Herald* of selling out to Tweed when, in fact, it was itself guilty.

Tweed was at the top of his form by then, convinced he had a long and fruitful career ahead of him. But he made a fatal mistake by refusing to pay former Sheriff Jimmy O'Brien the quarter of a million dollars he claimed he had earned while performing the duties of his office. Tweed had just successfully rewritten the City Charter, and the Board of Audit ruled that Jimmy's fee was for work performed under the old rules and was, therefore, invalid. O'Brien threatened to tell all he knew, but the Board, thinking he probably couldn't prove anything anyway, decided to save the City's money. Then, a few months later, the City Auditor was killed in an accident and O'Brien quietly installed a close friend of his in the vacant job. It didn't take the new auditor long to notice some astronomical bills for things like window shades and plasterwork for a new courthouse the City was building. He copied parts of the ledger for O'Brien, who encouraged him to keep up the good work.

When he had accumulated enough evidence, the ex-Sheriff took the copies to *The New York Times*, which began publishing them. Slippery Dick Connolly was dispatched to the *Times* office to offer its owner,

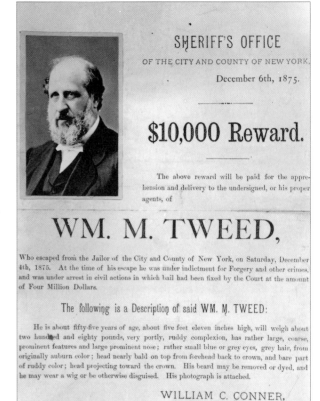

SHERIFF'S OFFICE
OF THE CITY AND COUNTY OF NEW YORK.

December 6th, 1875.

$10,000 Reward.

The above reward will be paid for the apprehension and delivery to the undersigned, or his proper agents, of

WM. M. TWEED,

Who escaped from the Jailor of the City and County of New York, on Saturday, December 4th, 1875. At the time of his escape he was under indictment for Forgery and other crimes, and was under arrest in civil actions in which bail had been fixed by the Court at the amount of Four Million Dollars.

The following is a Description of said WM. M. TWEED:

He is about fifty-five years of age, about five feet eleven inches high, will weigh about two hundred and eighty pounds, very portly, ruddy complexion, has rather large, coarse, prominent features and large prominent nose; rather small blue or grey eyes, grey hair, from originally auburn color; head nearly bald on top from forehead back to crown, and bare part of ruddy color; head projecting toward the crown. His beard may be removed or dyed, and he may wear a wig or be otherwise disguised. His photograph is attached.

WILLIAM C. CONNER,
Sheriff.

George Jones, $5 million to leave town. Jones informed him that he liked New York and intended to stay. Tweed couldn't believe it. He had never met a man who couldn't be bought. And just to prove it, he sent a banker friend to *Harper's Weekly* with an offer of $100,000 for cartoonist Thomas Nast to use to further his art career in Europe. Nast seemed interested. "Do you think I could get $200,000?" he asked. The answer was yes, which Nast countered with an appeal for $500,000. The banker assured him he could get that much and then Nast tossed him out of the office with a message for Tweed to the effect that all he wanted was to see him behind bars.

Mayor Hall refused any comment, but he barred *The Times* and *Harper's Weekly* from the public schools, cancelled orders for Harper textbooks and banned City employees from eating in the restaurant in the *Times* building. Then he made a tactical mistake. He ordered the City Buildings Department to sue *The Times* because its building was located on former City

As a worldwide search for Mr. Tweed got underway (facing page right), folks began looking carefully at strangers (facing page left). Up in Central Park, a woman who obviously didn't seem to need the $10,000 reward (left) thought it was worth asking which way the Boss might have gone.

land that had been sold at a low price to a church, which subsequently resold it to the newspaper. It was an illegal transaction, according to the Mayor, but his move to set things right kindled a fire under other newspapers all over the country, and even *The Times's* fiercest competitors, at least the ones not owned by Tweed, rose to the defense of free speech.

It was the last gasp of the Tweed Ring. Ironically, the accounts were published during the summer, when many of *The Times's* readers were out of town,

and those who weren't were more concerned with the weather than crooked politics. But by September, Tweed's scramble to discredit the report had reached desperate proportions and by then it was too late. He said in his defense that "Nine out of ten either know me or I know them; women and children you may include." It was true. All New York knew Boss Tweed and now they knew him for what he was.

Mayor Hall claimed that it was all the fault of the Republicans and General Grant. Slippery Dick Connolly

They didn't call New York the Big Apple during the Great Depression, but apples were a big source of income for many, including some men of the cloth (facing page).

Among the legacies of Tammany Mayor Fernando Wood was Central Park. When the 59th to 72d Street section was eliminated, he reinstated it and ordered work begun before he could be overruled. The aldermen were surprised at the sudden public spiritedness of the Mayor, but they let him have his way.

Former fireman William Tweed was the man for whom the term "graft" might have been invented. Like the railroad bosses, he made no secret of his dubious activities, but, his popularity notwithstanding, he was convicted of fellony. The engraving (left) shows Boss Tweed being examined by a committee of aldermen.

withdrew $4 million-worth of Government bonds from the City Treasury and then took his case to Samuel J. Tilden, a well-known reformer, who advised him to appoint an assistant who would take over the Comptroller's office in his name. When the assistant, a Tilden man, arrived, Connolly stepped aside and an armed guard was set up to protect the books. With that, Tilden was in control. Three years later he became an anti-Tammany Governor of New York and, in 1876, the Democratic candidate for President of the United States.

He owed it all to William Marcy Tweed. Tilden had been a loyal Tammany man before Tweed arrived on the scene, but turned his attention to other things when he glimpsed the future. Now the future was his, and he began building for it at the State Democratic Convention in 1871. Tweed had been discredited by then, but if he was down he was surely not out. The

Erie Railroad obligingly gave free passes to New York street-gang members so they could get to Rochester to make sure the Boss got what he wanted. The tactic nearly worked. Every candidate nominated for the State Legislature was a Tweed loyalist, but the reformers countered with their own slate. The reform candidates won easily in the election. All but one. Tweed kept his oversize chair in the Senate chamber.

But a few days after the election, Brains Sweeny, citing poor health, moved to Canada; Oakey Hall elegantly disavowed himself of any involvement. Slippery Dick Connolly had already slipped over to the other side, and Mr. Tweed was left without a friend in the world.

A few weeks later, Tweed appeared in the courthouse that had been the subject of the published secret accounts. It was the tip of the iceberg of the Great Man's enterprises, but enough to make him infamous. Nobody ever knew exactly what the building had cost, but a conservative estimate put the bill at $12.2 million, four times the cost of the Houses of Parliament, which were built in London at the same time. A grand jury indicted Tweed on 120 counts, ranging from forgery to false pretenses, and he was arrested on December 16, 1872. He applied for bail, but the judge, even though he owed his job to Tweed, refused to grant him even temporary freedom. The former Boss then took his case to the State Supreme Court and to his old crony Judge Barnard, who released him on a $5,000 bond.

He was given a speedy trial, but the jury couldn't agree on a verdict, and it was charged that they had been bribed. The prosecution hired detectives to watch over the jury at the second trial and it took almost no discussion among them to reach a unanimous verdict of guilty. On the day of sentencing, one of Tweed's seven lawyers made such an emotional plea for mercy that he was forced to cut his speech short because he was choked with tears. But the judge wasn't impressed. He fined Tweed $12,500 and sentenced him to twelve years in jail.

When he arrived at the Tombs prison in Manhattan to begin his sentence, Tweed identified himself in the register as a "statesman," and was ushered off to a cell that had been carpeted in anticipation of his tenancy. It had been furnished with a leather lounge, five chairs for visitors and a rocker for his own comfort. All of his jailors owed their jobs to the former Boss.

Tweed spent a year behind bars, during which time he was frequently allowed to go home for dinner with his family. Then, on the evening of December 5, 1875, Mr. Tweed didn't come back. During the visit with his

If the politics of the tenement neighborhoods weren't exactly clean, the local housewives did their best to keep their families clean. Meanwhile, Honest John Kelly (right) kept City Hall clean of scandal.

family, he managed to slip out of the house. It isn't easy for a six-foot-tall, three-hundred-pound man to vanish into thin air, but William M. Tweed accomplished it that night. It was later discovered that he had had help in the person of a fellow prisoner who had made elaborate arrangements to get him out of the country. After a long stopover in New Jersey, a brief stay on Staten Island and a sojourn in the Florida Everglades, he was spirited off to Havana, where he boarded a ship bound for Spain. But for all his careful planning, Tweed's benefactor had neglected to secure a Spanish visa. Meanwhile, Tweed's old pal Oakey Hall had made a sabre-rattling speech in favor of Cuban independence, which made the Spanish authorities suspicious of anybody who might be a New Yorker, especially if they had been to Havana recently. They didn't realize who this particular New Yorker was, but, acting on a tip from the U.S. State Department, and armed with a Thomas Nast cartoon of the Tammany Tiger, they took him into custody and notified the Americans that they had captured "Autelme Twid," the notorious kidnapper.

He arrived home a few weeks later, reduced to 160 pounds, but happy, he said, to be back in New York. His little vacation had cost him $60,000. He became the star witness in cases against other Tammany braves after that, always for the promise that his own sentence would be reduced. But when the promises weren't kept, he refused to testify at any more trials and, in a last act of defiance, asked the prosecutors what they thought they could do about it. They couldn't jail him for contempt of court, he reminded them, because he was already in jail. But he wouldn't be there much longer. On his way back from court that day he contracted pneumonia. Two weeks later he was dead.

Six months later, A. Oakey Hall stood trial for his transgressions, which he denied, and was found not guilty. He finished his term as Mayor and then went on

the stage as the star of a drama about innocence rewarded, which he wrote himself. He later became chief of the London Bureau of the *New York Herald*. Judge George Barnard was impeached, and neither Brains Sweeny nor Slippery Dick Connolly were ever heard from again.

However, in spite of the scandals and the reformers, the Tammany Tiger wasn't dead. It wasn't even caged. It was being tamed by Honest John Kelly.

Tweed had left the door wide open for the reformers to take over, and after the election of 1871, there were more Tammany men in Canada and Europe than in office. But Honest John Kelly had just come back from Europe, where he had spent three years distanced from Tweed and his cronies. The newly elected Mayor, William Havemeyer, welcomed John back with a letter that accused him of being worse than Tweed. "One honest spot in your character would be a relief," he said. Honest John just bided his time.

When it seemed most people had forgotten the

Boss Tweed may have been one of New York's worst rogues. But he had help from "Brains" Sweeney (left), Tammany's Albany lobbyist, and "Slippery Dick" Connolly (right), boss of the city's biggest Irish ward.

When Tweed went to jail, Tammany's reins were turned over to reformer Honest John Kelly, who once took a man to court for saying he wasn't really honest.

The last dramas of Tammany Hall were played out at its elegant wigwam on 17th Street, across from Union Square.

Tweed affair, Kelly invented a new scandal for them. The reformers had reached down into the ranks and replaced some Tammany-appointed election inspectors with their own men. Kelly filed misdemeanor charges against the police commissioners, and even though they had the Elegant Oakey Hall as their attorney, they lost the case as well as their jobs, and the reform Mayor lost the confidence of many of his constituents, who decided that they had just traded one gang of thieves for another.

Mayor Havemeyer died not long after that, as he was on his way to court to defend himself in a libel suit brought against him by Honest John after His Honor had challenged Kelly's honesty in public. Even though Tilden and his reformers were blocking the way on one hand and various powerful Tammanyites on the other, Honest John decided it was time to take control of the Wigwam and restore its power. And from 1872 until he died in 1886, Honest John Kelly had complete control, not only of the organization, but of the city's

government, too.

Honest John had never liked Tweed, and he liked his style even less. When he remade Tammany in his own image, it became an efficient machine, more powerful than it had ever been and with all of its power concentrated in a single person. It was a very simple system that had influence in every ward. Each was run by a district leader, who knew everybody in the neighborhood and was always on hand if anyone needed help. They organized picnics in summer and dances in winter, they sponsored athletic events and even provided cultural uplift. If anything good happened in a New York City neighborhood in the second half of the 19th century, chances are a Tammany district leader was behind it.

As George Washington Plunkitt pointed out, they gave their constituents opportunities so they wouldn't have to trouble them with political arguments. "I don't send them campaign literature," he said. "That's rot. People can get all the political stuff they want to read

Tammany had complete control of all city employees, from sanitation men to police officers (right) to police precinct captains (below). Among the secrets of its success was its regular distribution of food and favors to the needy poor. Even when others got the spirit at Christmas time (facing page), the people never forgot their year-round friends, especially on election day.

in the papers. Who reads speeches nowadays anyhow? It's bad enough to listen to them." He also pointed out that Tammany's charity was delivered quickly when it was needed most, and there was never a question asked. Not even, "how did you vote in the last election?" "I don't care if they're Republican or Democrat," said Plunkitt. "It's philanthropy. But it's politics, too. Mighty good politics."

Kelly was also careful to keep the Hall swept clean of scandal, and he succeeded. He had $500,000 in the bank when he died, but after Mayor Havemeyer, no one ever accused John Kelly of being anything but honest. His legacy was a new image for Tammany and an organization the like of which New York had never seen before. In any field.

But a tiger purring or a tiger snarling is still a tiger. And in 1892, a half-dozen years after Honest John Kelly presumably went to heaven, the Reverend Dr. Charles H. Parkhurst mounted the pulpit of the influential Madison Square Church and announced that "There is

not a form under which the devil disguises himself that so perplexes us ... as the polluted harpies that, under the pretense of governing this city, are feeding day and night on its quivering vitals."

The next day Tammany reverted to type. It denied the charge. Worse, it said that "a loose idea in a man's head is a dangerous thing. It rattles around until it drives the poor man crazy." John Kelly would probably have ignored the minister, and his parishioners would probably have gone right on sleeping through his sermons. But in 1892, Tammany was run by Richard Croker, who had set Tammany's morals back a hundred years by combining the organization of a Kelly with the avarice of a Tweed. And he was better at both than either of them.

Dr. Parkhurst had a right to be shocked. But his target wasn't as much Tammany Hall as the Police Department, although both institutions were inseparable in the '90s. No police officer ever got a promotion without a payoff, and if a man decided he

didn't want a promotion, he was moved from bad precincts to worse precincts until he changed his mind. The system, perfected by the efficient Croker, was worth some $7 million a year to Tammany and its sachems. The men on the beat, meanwhile, were paid off by local businessmen, legitimate or otherwise. And that is what upset Dr. Parkhurst.

The day after he fired his first broadside, Parkhurst was denounced in every newspaper in the city. Even Joseph Pulitzer's *New York World* warned him that he ought to study God's commandment about not bearing false witness. A week later, Croker arranged to have the minister hauled into court to prove his allegations. Parkhurst couldn't and the judge's decision was that he was guilty of stirring up the citizenry with an unwarranted feeling of distrust toward their elected officials.

That should have been the end of it, but the slur was more than the pastor could bear and he began touring the city visiting brothels and opium dens,

The housing crisis of the 1890s (above) makes the problems of a hundred years later seem simple. A century earlier, the city had been like a country town, with a cattle market on Fifth Avenue at 44th Street (facing page).

hoisting glasses of beer in waterfront bars and taking notes as he watched police officers doing the same things. He hired a private detective to accompany him, and the man later reported that he was forever asking him to "show me something worse." It wasn't hard. There was evil at every turn and the detective said that the Presbyterian minister "really went at his slumming work as if his heart was in his tour."

After several nights of building his case against debauchery, Dr. Parkhurst made his report in the form of a sermon to his congregation and to hundreds of interested New Yorkers who packed the Madison Square Church to the rafters. He had also hired four private detectives to visit as many saloons as possible

that were violating the Sunday closing law. It was a part of the investigation that he couldn't take care of himself because he was otherwise engaged on Sunday mornings. They managed to hit 254 of them in a single morning and presented the crusader with sworn affidavits that they had consumed a glass of beer in each of them. When Dr. Parkhurst appeared in his pulpit on March 13, he had their reports to add to his own. After his lurid description of the things he had seen and his brandishing of the documents he claimed would prove it, he drew back and said: "What are you going to do about it?".

Some citizens were shocked. But the most common reaction was to echo Richard Croker's observation that decent people should be outraged that a man of the cloth would visit dens of iniquity and even spend money in them. Even the President of the Society for the Prevention of Vice was scandalized and said, "Was it not an awful thing for a clergyman to do?". Even other ministers condemned him. The following Sunday, some churchgoers were told that "if Dr. Parkhurst wanted to see nude women, he should have had the good sense not to flaunt it before the public. And, anyway, he might have omitted the beer."

But the foreman of the Grand Jury in session that month was among the people who thought something ought to be done. He secured the minister's papers and the jury indicted the perpetrators named in them. Then they called the four commissioners who ran the Police Department. They were quickly dismissed for lack of evidence. They got the message, though, and fired the Department's chief inspector, whose replacement closed all seven thousand of the saloons that had been violating the blue laws. He also reassigned every police captain to a different precinct. Then he called a press conference and announced that the finest police department in the world was finer than ever. He also casually mentioned that there was a brothel across the Square from Dr. Parkhurst's church. But he didn't explain why he hadn't shut it down.

And that, apparently, was that. New Yorkers were titillated by vice trials for the rest of the spring and summer, but the presidential election campaign of 1892 distracted them, and in November they elected another Tammany hack as their mayor. They also sent a solid Tammany slate to the State Legislature. Dr.

CHAPTER 8

Life back in the "Good Old Days" included family bicycle outings on unpaved streets (right), treats from the granddaddy of the Good Humor Man, and Sunday excursions out to Coney Island (facing page) to ride on the Cannon Coaster for an answer to the question on its sign: "Will she throw her arms around your neck and yell?".

Parkhurst kept on railing against vice, but no one at City Hall or in Albany was listening.

Things changed after the 1893 election when Republicans took control of the Legislature and formed a commission to look into the minister's charges. Tammany men scoffed that Republican Boss Thomas C. Platt was looking for a way to get his finger into the city pie, and that the upstate farmers turned legislators were looking for a little excitement in their otherwise dull lives. But just to make the commission's work a little harder, they rounded up small-time lawbreakers and advised the bigger ones that they ought to move elsewhere until the heat was off. Most went to Chicago, but it was already too late for the Police Department to cover its tracks.

The hearings lasted seven months and there was hardly a dull day among them. New Yorkers heard lurid testimony from prominent madams and depressing details from abortionists; they learned the tricks of confidence men and looked into the lives of immigrants, who were arriving in the city at the rate of 18,000 a month. Every one of the nearly 700 witnesses who testified had one thing in common: part of their cost of living was paying off the police.

The result was the formation of a new police board which included a young public-spirited citizen named Theodore Roosevelt, who kept the department honest until 1897, when he moved on to bigger things. A dozen high police officials were indicted for their crimes, but eventually restored to their old jobs. Hundreds more took early retirement.

Meanwhile, in November 1897, the Tammany candidate for mayor, Robert A. Van Wyck, was elected in a landslide and excited citizens snake danced through the streets chanting, "Well, well, well, reform has gone to hell!"

Van Wyck was Richard Croker's personal choice, and with his election the Boss was more powerful than ever. But there were ambitious men in the ranks who thought of him as a tyrant and were beginning to say so. Nonetheless, Croker was confident and began spending more and more time at his castle in Ireland or at race tracks in England, running the City of New York by way of the Atlantic Cable.

But when his hand-picked candidate for governor, Mayor Van Wyck's brother, was defeated at the polls by Theodore Roosevelt in 1898, and Tammany lost City Hall to Seth Low in 1901, Croker decided it was time to retire. He moved to Ireland, where he bred racehorses and bulldogs. At the age of seventy-three, he married a twenty-three-year-old woman who claimed to be a direct descendant of the Indian chief, Sequoyah, and who had made a name for herself in a Wild West show during which she appeared on a white horse singing the national anthem in Cherokee. It was only fitting, she said, that she should be the wife of the chief

Today's restoration at South Street Seaport doesn't quite match what was there a century ago (left). But then, Fifth Avenue in front of the Plaza Hotel (above) doesn't look quite the same, either.

CHAPTER 8

Among the men who put America on wheels, Edward Henry Harriman and his sons were giants. Harriman also developed an early New York suburb at Tuxedo Park, and though it wasn't open to all, the idea opened doors to thousands of children of Mulberry Bend (facing page).

of Tammany Hall. When the chief died six years later, the former Indian maiden was left with $5 million and a castle in Ireland.

Tammany Hall was left in the hands of Charles Francis Murphy, a former saloon keeper, who became the most efficient Boss the Hall had ever known. He took the sachems out of the seamier businesses that had supported them in the past and encouraged them to get into legitimate fields like contracting and trucking, where their influence could earn even more money legally. He also exacted tribute from corporations looking for ways to bend city regulations. Everybody connected with Tammany Hall earned respectability and fortunes beyond their wildest dreams. As Lincoln Steffans pointed out, "If Tammany could be incorporated and all its earnings gathered up and paid out in dividends, the stockholders would get more than the New York Central bond and stockholders, more than the Standard Oil stockholders, and the controlling clique would wield a power equal to that of the United States Steel Company." They owed it all to Charlie Murphy.

Tammany still rigged elections, and some of the braves got out of hand once in a while, but Murphy taught them the value of a low profile and they learned their lessons well. He was neither an easy man to know nor to deal with, and that was exactly the way he wanted it. When W. Averell Harriman, the former Governor of New York, came home from his assignment as Ambassador to the Soviet Union, he was asked if he found it difficult to deal with Josef Stalin. "Not after dealing with Charlie Murphy," he said. When Murphy died, in 1924, Tammany knew it would never see a man like him again.

YOU CAN'T STOP PROGRESS, BUT YOU CAN TRY

The power of Tammany Hall moved in strange ways. Consider the crusade of Alderman Peter McGuiness. "I seen it coming as far back as 1928," he told a reporter. "I seen the machine age coming. So far as I know, I was the first to speak about it. One night at the clubhouse, I said to the gentlemen there, 'Look here, gentlemen, suppose you got ten tons of bricks to haul ten miles. You got to use three teams, six horses, three drivers, and it's going to take you a day to do it. That's a ten-hour day I'm talking about. With a truck you could make eight trips in a ten-hour day. That's throwing about twenty-four men out of work'." He proposed, and they all solemnly backed him, that they put a stop to the activities of the U.S. Patent Office. "Just notify them that they can't O.K. any more of these machines. We got to put a stop to the machine age." The Patent Office was too busy to respond to his request.

BALANCING THE BOOKS

In 1901, when *Cosmopolitan* magazine had a slightly different view of what makes the world go 'round than it does today, its publisher, William Randolph Hearst, raised the question of what was to become of what was generally acknowledged to be the world's greatest fortune.

Pointing out that John Davison Rockefeller's millions would soon pass to his son, John D. Rockefeller, Jr., *Cosmopolitan* warned that "... the power of the money covers so vast a territory that a man inheriting such a fortune has it within his power to revolutionize the world or use it so evilly as to retard civilization for a quarter of a century."

The world would have to wait forty-one years before the founder of the Rockefeller fortune left his son more than $500 million and all the power Hearst had warned his readers about. But it had been given plenty of clues along the way that Mr. Junior, as the young man was known, did not have an evil thought in his head and that, though he would follow in his father's footsteps and the world would be revolutionized, civilization would not be in the least retarded.

The elder Rockefeller enjoyed the unenviable reputation as the ultimate barbarian of the business world, in spite of the fact he was a man with all the homely attributes Americans profess to admire. He was a faithful churchgoer, a Sunday school teacher, in fact, who ungrudgingly gave ten percent of his income to the church, even when his income was only $3.50 a week. He neither drank nor smoked, and was visibly offended by profanity. He was never happier than in the bosom of his family, a household that included his own mother, his mother-in-law and his spinster sister-in-law, all of whom he adored. He enjoyed playing children's games with his three daughters and taught his only son how to swim and skate.

John D. Rockefeller's problem was that he had built the world's greatest fortune without the dubious business ethics and flamboyance of the 19th-century robber barons, which resulted in some rather dull copy. But there were enough chinks in his armor to provide grist for the mills of tabloid journalists and the so-called muckrakers. He never confirmed or denied their attacks, which convinced most people that he probably had something to hide. It was easy to understand. The man had not only accumulated a fortune, but, in the process, had elbowed competition out of the way, sometimes unmercifully, to create America's first trust, an organization with all the earmarks of a monopoly. It was the country's most

When John D. Rockefeller moved to New York from Cleveland, few people even noticed. They were busy having a good time at places like the Savoy Ballroom. Mr. Rockefeller's idea of a good time was Sunday drives with a pair of fine horses (after church, of course).

powerful industrial entity and the first business enterprise to carry the American flag abroad. Even if America at large had been told that John D. Rockefeller lived an exemplary life, they probably wouldn't have believed it anyway. It didn't seem possible that an honest man could accumulate a fortune that one observer said was equal to the amount that would have been accumulated if Adam had made the decision to deposit $500 a day in the Garden of Eden Bank and his descendants had continued the practice every day of their lives right up to the present.

But it was. John D. Rockefeller considered himself to be a gentleman, convinced that God had ordained him to build his fortune, and if he ever strayed from the straight and narrow in his business dealings, he was just as convinced it was God's will.

As a boy he was determined to make good, and when he graduated from high school in Cleveland,

139

Rockefeller once said that "Only through pruning could the American Beauty rose have been developed." The press never let him forget it.

Ohio, he couldn't bear the idea of spending four more years with school books. He decided instead to spend them working with the ledger books of one of Cleveland's most successful commodity merchants. He kept a ledger book of his own, which later became a tradition with his son and grandsons, recording every penny he earned or spent. He left his first job within three years, when his employers refused him a raise and, after borrowing capital from his father, went into business for himself. Two years later, the debt paid, young Rockefeller and his partner divided a profit of $1,700 between them. He was on his way.

The Civil War was creating instant millionaires at the time, and Cleveland's share of them seemed destined to come from an 1858 oil bonanza in nearby Pennsylvania. It was just the ticket for a young, eager man like Rockefeller. But he was never a man to jump quickly into the unknown and, though he invested in the oil business, he was still convinced that there was no future in it.

But in the Cleveland of the 1860s, which had direct transportation links to both the oil fields and the Port of New York, oil was king. Rockefeller finally got the message and built a small refinery. He also rented warehouse space to other refiners, and that is when he

When the Brooklyn Bridge opened in 1883, the fireworks display lasted a solid hour without letup.

The day the Brooklyn Bridge opened, the Statue of Liberty's torch was on display in Madison Square. Three years later, New Yorkers had to climb up a ladder inside the arm to get the same close-up look.

CHAPTER 9

The New York Stock Exchange, synonymous with Wall Street, is actually on Broad Street.

discovered that the men getting rich on oil were disorganized and wasteful. Both qualities were anathema to John D. Rockefeller, and he began remaking the oil business in his own image. He noticed that the barrels others were using tended to be leaky, so he built a factory to make better ones for his own company. He found greed in the oil fields and, where others expanded and overproduced, he cautiously controlled production, buying oil when it was cheap and shipping it when the price went up. Within a year, at the age of twenty-six, he outbid his partners for control of the company, which was already twice as profitable as its nearest competitor.

Then he began a search for new partners. First among them was Henry M. Flagler, a man as reckless as Rockefeller was conservative.

Flagler was a natural salesman who was especially adept at dealing with the railroad men, the key to any successful oil enterprise. The railroaders weren't too happy with the oil men because their shipments were unpredictable. When they overproduced, they filled every available tank car, and then, often within days, as they stopped to catch their breath, all the rolling stock was sidetracked. The combination of Flagler's salesmanship and Rockefeller's careful planning convinced the railroads that they could provide steady traffic, with the result that they had a monopoly on every tank car within miles of Cleveland. They were able to guarantee so much business, in fact, that they secured a rebate on their freight rates.

With well-organized production and lower costs, Rockefeller was able to secure financing for a brand-new company. It was formed at the height of a depression, but the newborn Standard Oil company turned the economy's problems into an advantage by investing in another scheme: a holding company that tied the railroads and the big refiners together in a cartel which controlled production and transportation. It was a closely kept secret, with Rockefeller and some trusted competitors conspiring with Jay Gould, W.H. Vanderbilt and the other railroad barons to handpick the participants. Those who weren't selected faced the choice of going out of business or selling out to Rockefeller.

He made no bones about telling them that if they didn't join him he would destroy them. Yet he never for a minute thought that crushing competition deviated from his Christian principles. In fact, he thought it was an act of charity. He told the small operators that Standard Oil stood ready to assume all the risks with nothing less in mind than to save the less businesslike in the industry from their inevitable downfall.

But the competition didn't want to be saved. Instead they joined together to fight the Standard Oil octopus. They agreed among themselves not to send any crude oil to Standard's refineries, but by the time they were all singing from the same songbook, they were too late. There were no refineries in Cleveland that Rockefeller hadn't quietly bought. He controlled more than a quarter of all the oil refineries in the country, in fact, and was working hard to swallow up the others. Within five years, Standard controlled all but a handful of America's oil refineries. In the process, Rockefeller gained control of the shippers who had come to depend on the company's business.

In the case of John D. Rockefeller, control is almost too mild a word. He routinely visited all of the company's plants unannounced, taking notes on how

The first stock trading in New York took place at the Tontine Coffee House at Wall and Water streets.

CHAPTER 9

Strolls through the Park in the '90s often led to the Mall for band concerts. The fresh air was kept fresher by a ban on smoking there.

Construction of the Brooklyn Bridge kept hundreds of men working for thirteen years. Roebling's masterpiece was a landmark in the field of bridge building, introducing a significant number of engineering "firsts."

they were being run and suggesting efficiencies to make them run better. He kept a close eye on his competition and used his organization to stamp them out. He authorized his sales people to introduce price cutting when it was necessary to become the only game in town. And if a price war didn't work, they weren't above manipulating a competitor's suppliers and bankers to get their message across. It was then that the press attacks began. The small businessmen driven to ruin by the Standard Oil giant became symbolic victims of corporate greed. But if Mr. Rockefeller felt stung by the accusations, he never showed it.

The trust he created encompassed forty different corporations, a dozen of which were owned directly by Standard Oil. But they were all so intricately interlocked that no one could prove who owned what. On the other hand, it was clear to everyone that the head of the octopus was John D. Rockefeller. It was only natural that such a man would move to New York.

The Rockefeller family left its mark all over New York. Riverside Church, which cost them $26 million in 1930, was one of their first monuments.

The empire was run from 26 Broadway, overlooking Bowling Green and the site of the original Fort Amsterdam. Though Rockefeller himself was its symbol, it was run by an incredible group of men who were later known as the "Standard Oil Gang." It included John D.'s brother, William, whose sons would eventually, through marriage, gain control of the First National City Bank; Henry Rogers, a self-made Wall Street millionaire; John Archbold, a former independent oil man who had led the fight to stop Rockefeller before he joined forces with him; Oliver Payne, whose father, a U.S. senator, joined forces with Rockefeller's boyhood friend, Senator Mark Hanna, to bestow Federal blessings on the company; Charles Pratt, a New York oil refiner who had thrown in his lot with the Standard; and, of course, the ever-present Henry Flagler. It was a group that inspired William Vanderbilt to claim "I have never come into contact with any class of men as smart and able as they are." Rockefeller couldn't have agreed more. "Find the man who can do the particular thing you want done and then leave him to do it unhampered" he said. It was an untraditional way to run a business in the 1890s, but it worked.

The company's best-selling product was kerosene, but it found uses for all the other petroleum by-products, too, and aggressively found world-wide markets for them. They had a use for everything they produced except gasoline, but progress in other fields would soon take care of that. The Standard Oil marketers were on top of each new refinement in the development of the internal combustion engine. Even before there were cars in some towns, Standard Oil had already established service stations for them. And when airplanes began flying, Standard's sales people were well-established on the ground floor.

Meanwhile, almost nobody believed that John D. Rockefeller was anything but evil. The richer he got, the more people believed it. He tried to disassociate himself from some of the scandals that involved his henchmen, but in the public mind Standard Oil was an extension of Rockefeller himself. What very few people knew, however, was that, as early as 1896, he had

The Wall Street facade of the Morgan Bank still has scars from an unsolved explosion in 1920. Thirty-three bystanders were killed and four hundred injured.

John D. Rockefeller and his sons lived in a row of fashionable houses on W. 54th Street off Fifth Avenue.

stopped working and had turned his attention from making money to giving it away.

The idea that American millionaires should follow the lead of the Medicis was brought to their attention in a widely read essay written by Andrew Carnegie in 1889. But Carnegie never gave away a dime without getting a dollar's worth of publicity in return. Like some modern businessmen, he made sure that his name became the name of institutions he funded. But John D. Rockefeller was as private in his philanthropies as he was in his business affairs. Even when there was publicity, it was sometimes turned against him. When he gave $100,000 to the Congregational Church, the gift was rejected with great fanfare on the grounds that it was "tainted money." What the Congregationalists neglected to say was that they had asked for the money in the first place. And when the furore died down they took it anyway.

Beyond being secretive, Rockefeller was also, as was typical, very well organized about his giving. Throughout his business career he had been

Andrew Carnegie was the first of the American millionaires to make philanthropy a way of life. Carnegie Hall, which he built for the New York Oratorio Society, cost him $2 million.

overwhelmed with requests for donations to various charities, and though he honored many of them, he finally hired a former Baptist minister, Frederick T. Gates, to separate the wheat from the chaff. Gates's first choice was to turn a Baptist theological seminary into the University of Chicago. Over the next dozen years, the transformation would cost Rockefeller more than $45 million, but he said he had never made a better investment. There would be hundreds more before the old man died in 1937, two years short of his hundredth birthday. But Gates had an even more important role. He was also put in charge of managing Rockefeller's personal finances. The man couldn't seem to stop making money. In the years after his retirement, his income quadrupled to more than $1 billion . And he owed much of it to Gates, who kept a close eye on his investments.

Though he considered himself retired, Rockefeller hadn't heard the last of the public outcry against himself and Standard Oil. When Theodore Roosevelt

After passing the bulk of his fortune to his son, John D. Rockefeller, Jr., in 1917, the founder of Standard Oil (pictured with his heir right) "retired" with only $20 million in his own name. But he was still an important man about town and even routine visits to the tailor were notable events.

CHAPTER 9

When the market crashed in 1929, millions of people who couldn't get to the bank in time lost their life savings. John D. Rockefeller, Jr. himself (below right) lost a fortune, but not all of it. He had just signed a 24-year lease, at $3.3 million a year, for the site of the future Rockefeller Center.

became president in 1901, he began attacking trusts and, in 1911, the battle culminated in a Supreme Court decision that Standard Oil must cease to exist. The corporation complied by breaking up into smaller companies, each of which respected the territorial rights of its cousins. In the process, the stockholders of the original company collectively earned a windfall of $200 million. It prompted Gates to warn Rockefeller that his fortune was growing much too fast. "You must distribute it faster than it grows," he warned, "if you do not, it will crush you."

The philanthropist had already established the Rockefeller Institute for Medical Research, now known as Rockefeller University, in New York, and he had provided the funds to set up the General Education Board, formed in 1901 to promote black education in the South. But his giving reached unprecedented heights in 1910 when he allocated $150 million to begin the Rockefeller Foundation, which would disburse money on a world-wide basis.

The Bible says that charity covers a multitude of

On Thursday, October 24, 1929, as the theatrical newspaper Variety put it, Wall Street laid an egg. And a lot of nest eggs became worthless pieces of paper.

sins. If the American public had seen John D. Rockefeller as a sinner, their attitude began to change. Many said it was because Rockefeller hired a PR man. Joseph Clarke was the second person in the history of American business to hold such a job. The first was Ivy Lee, who left his job with the Pennsylvania Railroad to become a Rockefeller man. Their job was simply defined. If any newspaper printed information detrimental to the man or the company, they dug up the new facts and sent a Standard Oil salesman to the newspaper's office with a demand to print what, in the company's eyes, was the true story. They also commissioned friendly biographies of the old man and sold serialization rights to magazines. It was a technique that had worked well for Ida Tarbell, Lincoln Steffens and others who raised a hue and cry against the company at the turn of the century, but most corporations still responded to such attacks with shrill screaming at stockholders' meetings or, like Rockefeller, they simply ignored the attacks.

Rockefeller knew what the Bible had to say about charity, but he had apparently missed the wisdom of the ancient Roman poet who said that charity begins at home. When his son, John D. Jr., graduated from college, he was immediately put on his father's payroll and went to work with Reverend Gates at 26 Broadway. His duties were vague, but he was made a board member of seventeen different corporations, including U.S. Steel, for the less-than-magnificent salary of $10,000 a year. The young man wrote a thank-you note to his father, saying, without any sign of tongue in cheek, "My breath was completely taken away by what you told me regarding my salary for the year." He went on to say that he didn't know how he could possibly be worth that much. He didn't, but his father did. Mr. Junior was a chip off the old block.

He had his father's eye for detail and his devotion to hard work. But he didn't have a stomach for the business world and decided early to follow in his father's footsteps as a philanthropist. The old man approved, and the combination of father and son and Frederick Gates became a formidable one. In the first

The Great Depression began with lines of confused depositors locked out of their banks.

Once the initial shock of the crash was over, Wall Street itself became comparatively deserted.

decade of the 20th century, Rockefeller gifts added up to more than $130 million, ten times as much as the old man had managed to give away in the previous ten years. And their giving became more creative. The elder Rockefeller had favored education, Gates leaned toward religious institutions, but John D. Jr. began encouraging the channeling of money into social welfare and public health programs. His father, meanwhile, began looking for ways to make the philanthropy world-wide as much of his company's profits had come from international marketing.

Then Mr. Junior discovered a new cause to occupy his attention. After Reverend Parkhust began preaching against sin in general and Tammany Hall in particular, in 1892, the city tried to clean up its act, but eventually it drifted back to its old evil ways, much "as a drunkard returns to his liquor," as one newspaper put it. In the election campaign of 1909, the issue that excited the voters was a charge that women were being lured into prostitution against their will. Tammany won the election in spite of it, but the problem, which earned the name "white slavery" during the campaign, wouldn't go away. Bowing to voter pressure, the city fathers called a special grand jury to investigate the problem. John D. Rockefeller, Jr. was made its foreman. He went protesting to the jury box, explaining to the judge that most men at least knew from private experience about the problem, but that he didn't have any such experience. He was, after all, a Sunday school teacher at the Madison Avenue Baptist Church. The judge told him that experience wasn't required. And over at Tammany Hall, the sachems just smiled. John D.

Rockefeller, Jr. was just the kind of man they were looking for; someone who was socially prominent, but inexperienced enough to be manipulated. They made the wrong choice. Once Mr. Junior accepted the post, he dedicated himself to it. He interviewed social workers and police officers, he read every book he could find on the subject of prostitution and consulted with public health authorities, many of whom worked for organizations Rockefeller money had established.

The grand jury's term was scheduled to end in a month, but Mr. Junior kept it alive for six months. When its work was finished, the judge refused to

Less than a mile from Wall Street, life on Mulberry Street went on as it had for a hundred years.

Life in the tenements of the Lower East Side began to improve when immigration quotas were established in the 1920s and slum clearance, begun at the same time, replaced crowded and dingy flats like these.

accept its findings so young Rockefeller challenged him in open court. The press, which hadn't taken much notice of the young millionaire, suddenly made a hero of him. The judge finally gave in and handed down dozens of indictments, but the Mayor refused to do anything about them, hoping, apparently, that the whole thing would blow over. It would have, but the former jury foreman didn't give up. In 1910, he enlisted the help of Jacob Schiff and Paul Warburg, two leading Jewish businessmen, and formed a committee of three to attack the problem on their own. It was the first alliance of Christians and Jews in the City of New York, establishing a pattern that hasn't changed since.

Their first target was the Jewish ghetto on the Lower East Side, where young immigrant women were especially vulnerable to white slavers. The combination of money and enthusiasm encouraged others to join the fight and eventually their activities extended to the creation of the Bureau of Social Hygiene, which was instrumental in cleaning up not only the problem of

It was a short walk from the ghetto to the financial district, and even though it would take a giant step to become part of it, some began taking their dreams there at a very early age.

"Let's have lunch!" has been the rallying cry of New York business for generations. But even though lunch was as cheap as five cents, many Depression-era businessmen settled for breadlines.

No matter how the economy behaves, hot summer days will always be inevitable, and if the bus for the Hamptons left without you, well, there were other ways to keep cool.

prostitution, but many of the other evils of the ghetto. It also led to Tammany's downfall in the election of 1913, and to Rockefeller's interest in reforming the city government. He didn't kill the Tammany tiger, but he made it wish it had never picked him for that grand jury.

After the First World War, Mr. Junior became more and more interested in international affairs. He also became fascinated by the idea of uniting the Christian religions, and donated nearly the entire cost of building Riverside Church in Upper Manhattan as a first step toward unity. Most importantly, in the 1920s he became an ardent supporter of the arts. A combination of that enthusiasm and the Great Depression that followed the 1929 stock market crash gave New York its most visible reminder that John D. Rockefeller, Jr.

CHAPTER 9

was one of the true giants of the city's history.

By the time the market crashed, the Rockefeller heir had brought his sons, John D. III and Nelson, into his organization. But though the family fortune held together during the Depression, it was clearly not a time for expansion of their philanthropies. Both young men chafed at the dim prospect, but fate had good things in store. In 1927, the trustees of the Metropolitan Opera decided to move their opera house from a neighborhood that had been taken over by the garment industry, and Mr. Junior was pleased to help. He was intensely interested in civic improvements, not to mention supporting the arts, and the Met's problem gave him a chance to satisfy both passions. It also gave him a means of upgrading the neighborhood surrounding his house on West 54th Street. He had acquired several parcels of land along Fifth and Sixth Avenues and was more than willing to donate them to the cause. But the bulk of the properties separating them were owned by Columbia University, which

At the height of the Great Depression, more than 75,000 men went to work every day to build Rockefeller Center.

158

wasn't at all interested in selling. Rockefeller's lawyers went to work to secure a long-term lease on the land. Having accomplished that, Mr. Junior had control of three full blocks of midtown real estate. He set up a corporation to develop it, with the new opera house as its centerpiece. It would be a means of financing the development, and a lure for businesses to relocate in what had been a run-down neighborhood. But the Opera's trustees dragged their feet, finally sending a message to Rockefeller that they wouldn't move unless he paid half the cost of their new building. He was

already committed to building on the site, but sent a message back that he wouldn't be blackmailed. He didn't give up hope that the opera company would eventually become his partner in the project, but the stock market crash had cost him hundreds of millions and he had invested $10 million in the development plan. When the Met finally said it wasn't interested, Mr. Junior went to work to pick up the pieces.

A less stubborn man would have walked away. The Depression made it foolhardy to plan office buildings in 1930, but, as Mr. Junior explained to a biographer,

For those who couldn't find jobs, home was a shack made of packing cases in the shadow of Riverside Church and Grant's Tomb.

159

The biggest of the Rockefeller Center buildings, RCA's 70-story headquarters, was ready for occupancy in 1930.

In 1930, automobile tycoon Walter Chrysler expressed his faith in coming good times by building the world's tallest building. A year later, the title was snatched away by the Empire State Building.

he had no alternative but to go forward. If nothing else, it was an expression of confidence that the economy would eventually recover. But in those days, even optimists like Rockefeller had secret doubts that it ever would. Denying that courage had anything to with it, he announced that he was going to fill the blocks along Fifth and Sixth Avenues between 48th and 51st Streets with a complex of office buildings. The taxes and rent on the land over the twenty-four-year term of the lease he had negotiated with Columbia amounted to some $90 million; the buildings would cost another $160 million, and the best guess was that rentals would bring in less than $8 million. But the guessers were wrong.

Raymond Hood, a key member of the team of architects hired to design the complex, went to Rockefeller with the idea that a former client of his, Radio Corporation of America, might be interested in renting huge amounts of space for its lusty young offspring, the National Broadcasting Company. Not only that, but RCA also owned RKO, a major movie company. The idea changed everything. RCA was very interested. By 1931 it had committed to $2.75 million a year in rentals for studio and office space and another

$1.5 million for theater space. As far as Rockefeller was concerned, the Depression was over.

Mr. Junior was also able, of course, to interest various offspring of Standard Oil to relocate in his complex, and his brother-in-law, the President of the Chase National Bank, agreed to lease space for no less than three bank branches. All of which made financing possible, even easy; Mr. Junior and his two sons began building Rockefeller Center.

After construction began, the Depression caught up with RCA, which scaled back its leases and eliminated two of the theaters it had planned. The Rockefellers turned that into an opportunity when they negotiated a contract with Samuel Rothafel, known as "Roxy," who ran a movie palace of the same name a block away, to oversee the building and operation of the grandest theater ever built, the 6,200-seat Radio City Music Hall. To a city still feeling the effects of hard times, it became a symbol of better days ahead. For thousands of construction workers, steady work on the theater and the five other buildings meant regular paychecks. It all added up to a new image for the Rockefellers. People finally began forgiving them for what they had considered to be the sins of the father.

161

A HOT TIME IN THE OLD TOWN

The consolidation of the five boroughs of New York in 1898 opened undreamed-of opportunities for politicians and businessmen alike. The whole country was prosperous at the turn of the century, but the expanding City of New York was clearly where the action was. As one writer pointed out, it was "undoubtedly on the road to becoming the most national and least suburban of American cities." It was also international, even then, and, as the business center of the world, it was completely dedicated to perking up the after-hours spirits of tired businessmen.

The party began every evening at six and went on past sunrise. Rich and poor met together for the first time to have a good time in hundreds of cabarets that featured small tables, big prices and strange dances with even stranger names, like the grizzly bear, the turkey trot and, yes, the big apple. The whole business was condemned from the city's pulpits and in its press. But the raillery fell on deaf ears. If dancing was sinful, so be it. It was fun.

When the curtain rose on the twentieth century, New Yorkers were dazzled with opportunities to be entertained. Fierce competition among theatrical giants

When a Constitutional amendment dried up the alcohol supply in 1919, some New Yorkers solved the problem by patronizing their neighborhood speakeasy (facing page). Others who could afford it took long ocean cruises beyond the reach of American laws.

like B.F. Keith and Edward Albee, William Morris, Martin Beck and the Shubert Brothers was making them into millionaires, and the stars who graced their lavish productions became legendary. New York had been a theater town since colonial days, but it had never been served a menu like the one entrepreneurs dished up after the 1905 season. What had been a Saturday night pastime suddenly demanded attention three or four nights a week. And New Yorkers were more than ready for the experience.

They laughed at mother-in-law jokes, cried over monologues about the old folks at home, and they gave rapt attention to dancers impersonating Salome shedding their seven veils one by one. And after the entertainment, audiences and cast members alike walked over to Rector's or Shanley's to tackle a giant lobster and look around the room for famous faces.

One of the big winners was Willie Hammerstein,

who earned a profit of $5 million with vaudeville bills at his Victoria Theater. The entertainers who graced his stage included a pair of girls who had shot and wounded a socialite. They didn't do much else, but Willie billed them as "the shooting stars," and sold out the house. He also presented the infamous Cherry Sisters, whom he advertised as "America's worst act," and sold eggs and vegetables in the lobby for the audiences to toss at them. Willie's greatest coup was bringing Evelyn Nesbit to the Victoria after her husband, Harry Thaw, shot the architect Stanford White. He paid her $3,500 a week to glide across the stage on a red velvet swing, and pocketed a profit of $10,000 a week for his trouble. In those days before air-conditioning, Willie lured summertime customers by placing a thermometer in a block of ice outside the theater along with a sign that said it registered the inside temperature. It didn't, but he made ticket buyers think it did by

Times Square was the place to be seen in those days, and to see a movie in surroundings that rivaled the great cathedrals of Europe.

If they don't look like G-men, don't be fooled! These minions of the law did their best to keep New York sober between 1920 and 1933.

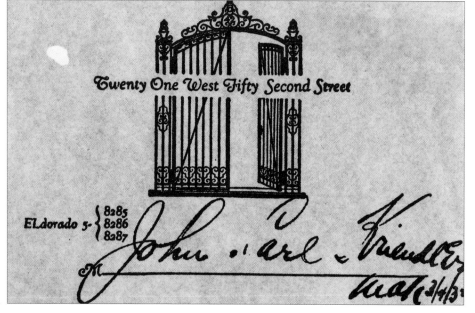

heating the elevator that took them up to his roof garden.

By 1907, theatergoers were distracted by something brand-new. Movies, the first of which were produced in New York, could provide a half-hour of escape for a nickel. Vaudeville producers added films to their bills to keep the audiences from leaving before the last act. But the legitimate theater men had to clean up their act and begin providing bigger stars in more lavish productions. It all conspired to make everybody more successful and a good bit wealthier.

Meanwhile, Americans were also entertaining themselves at home around a piano in the parlor, and New York was providing them with songs to sing. The block of 28th Street west of Broadway became known as Tin Pan Alley, as men like George M. Cohan, Irving Berlin and Gus Edwards were grinding out sheet music that sold as many as a million copies apiece, earning them a five-cent royalty on each and every one. Among the big money-makers were "I Just Can't Make My Eyes Behave," "If You Talk In Your Sleep, Don't

Mention My Name," and "Be My Little Baby Bumble Bee." And the biggest hit of 1905 was "Will You Love Me In December As You Did In May?". It was written by a young man named James J. Walker, who in 1926 would become Mayor of the City of New York.

Jimmy arrived at City Hall during an era known by

Revenue agents made regular raids on speakeasies and poured the booze into the sewers. But most establishments, like the 21 Club, stayed open anyway.

167

CHAPTER 10

the single word, "Prohibition." He said he had heard about the Constitutional Amendment to make drinking illegal, but added, "I wonder when it is going to start." It officially started at midnight on January 16, 1920, and from that moment the singing and dancing seemed doomed. The big and famous restaurants in the theater district were forced to close their doors. Murray's Roman Gardens on 42nd Street was turned into a flea circus, the dining room at the Plaza Hotel became an automobile showroom. Cabarets vanished, the saloons of the Tenderloin ceased to exist. But the drinking never stopped. Izzy Einstein, the Federal agent in charge of rooting them out, estimated that there were about one hundred thousand speakeasies selling liquor in brownstones, lofts and cellars all over New York. He was a dedicated man and managed to arrest 4,932 offenders after worming his way into their establishments in a variety of disguises ranging from ice man or waiter to thirsty out-of-town buyer. But even a dedicated public servant like Izzy couldn't stem the tide.

If anyone personified the spirit of the 1920s, it was Mayor James J. Walker, who every now and then was seen during the daytime performing such mayoral functions as dedicating traffic lights.

CHAPTER 10

Mah-jongg took the city by storm in the '20s and fashionable women learned the rules from radio broadcasts. Others took advantage of their new freedom with more strenuous pursuits.

There was plenty to keep everyone busy on Broadway in the '20s, much of it created by entrepreneur Oscar Hammerstein (left).

Many of the speakeasies were high-class operations run as private clubs. Some required membership cards, but most admitted anyone who knew the password, which was often easily available from the cop on the beat. Inside, patrons were served with what pretended to be imported Scotch or gin. Actually, the stuff began life as imported liquor, usually brought down from Canada in fast speedboats called rum-runners and stashed in waterfront warehouses. However, the warehouses were also factories where new bottles were manufactured and filled with a product made by adding water, food coloring and a little raw alcohol to the original liquor. The process created at least three new bottles for every one slipped past the Coast Guard, and the cutting factories also had printing presses to produce counterfeit labels that made the contents seem legitimate. But no one was fooled, and speakeasy patrons began arriving with their own pocket flasks, ordering, as many New Yorkers do these days, just water. The speakeasy operators obliged. A cocktail cost a dollar, but a bottle of water was twice the price.

Most speakeasies also operated as restaurants, usually Italian, but sometimes French, and functioned as pre-theater gathering places. After the theater, the fashionable usually went in search of nightclubs for some serious illegal drinking. It was a moveable feast because Federal agents were especially adept at finding them. But the nightclub was a high-profit innovation, and the closing of one usually meant the opening of another by the same management. It was the idea of a former chorus girl named Texas Guinan after she was invited to sing at a speakeasy and decided never to go back to the theater. Her partner, a former taxi fleet operator, studied the clubs of London and Paris and brought the best of both to the glittering El Fey Club.

CHAPTER 10

It was an instant hit, popular with middle-class businessmen as well as gangsters, theatrical personalities and the socially prominent. It was a fascinating mix that made Guinan the best-known woman in town. Before long, she had nearly one hundred competitors. It didn't matter. There were plenty of customers to go around. But to help prevent them from getting any ideas about club-crawling, she introduced another New York institution, the cover charge. It also increased the profit potential from those who preferred to soak up the atmosphere and not the gin.

Guinan also invented another way of making money by hiring three girls to work the room, one selling cigarettes, another souvenir dolls and a third corsages, usually a gardenia that turned brown almost as soon as the $5 price was paid. No one was forced to buy from them, but any man who didn't was loudly branded a cheapskate. But the nightclubs of the '20s were clearly no place for cheapskates. *The Tribune* reported that a party of four at Texas Guinan's could

expect to spend about $1,300 for an evening of fun and frolic. It was not for nothing that Miss Guinan welcomed them to her establishment by saying "Hello, suckers!"

Apart from the show put on by the patrons, and the occasional drama of a police raid, all of the clubs provided entertainment with stars of the caliber of Jimmy Durante, Fred Astaire, Paul Whiteman and Helen Morgan. And the entertainment was city-wide. When black stars like Eubie Blake began appearing at the downtown clubs, fun-seekers began going up to Harlem for more. They found Ethel Waters there, and Bojangles Robinson, not to mention Duke Ellington and Louis Armstrong.

One of the chroniclers of the era, Walter Winchell, wrote in the *Daily Mirror* that it was a time "when we saps believed a rising stock market was taking us nearer to heaven on earth; when everybody thought the lottery had more prizes than tickets; when flaming youth and the lights of Broadway were the vogue, and the torch of the Statue of Liberty was a burned-out

Theatergoers line up in Times Square for bargain tickets even today. In 1928, they bought them from stars like Eva Le Gallienne. After the theater, they flocked to clubs made famous by Texas Guinan (facing page).

electric bulb." It was a time that was exactly right for the election of James J. Walker to lead the parade. After he was elected, Jimmy asked to have his salary as Mayor raised, but when the request was turned down, he said, "Think how much it would cost if I worked full time."

Gentleman Jim may not have shown up at City Hall every day, but he managed to keep in the public eye in his own way. He said that the greatest sin was going to bed on the same day you got up, and he worked hard at avoiding it. He had a wife he rarely saw and a girlfriend who was seen everywhere with him. "I make my private life pretty public," he said. "I don't sneak in and out of restaurants, nightclubs, the fights at the Garden, the opening nights at the Broadway theaters. I take her with me everywhere, always where the lights are brightest. I have nothing to hide."

It turned out he did. When he ran for a second term in 1929 he won by a two-to-one margin. But only a few

If an ice cream cone didn't cool you off, you could go over to Marcus Loew's American Theater for ten acts of vaudeville, including Mme. Sarah Bernhardt. At intermission, you could go up to the roof garden to catch the Hudson River breeze. All for a quarter.

Mayor Walker won his second term by a two-to-one margin after reminding the voters that loyalty was at the heart of democracy. A few months later, the scandals of his first administration caught up with him and he was forced to resign.

After the Wall Street Crash, New Yorkers and labor leaders began demonstrating against the "high cost of living." But as Al Jolson had told them back in '27, "You ain't heard nothin' yet!"

days before the election, the Wall Street crash wiped out some $32 billion in stock holdings, and in New York City more than 100,000 people were out of work. The fun was over and the fun-loving Mayor didn't have any more answers. It had been charged during the campaign that high city officials were in league with the gangsters who kept the illegal liquor flowing, and Franklin D. Roosevelt, who had been elected Governor of New York the previous year, ordered an official investigation. The commission, headed by Judge Samuel Seabury, worked for twenty months looking into the charges. They uncovered corruption everywhere they looked. The Mayor himself, it transpired, had collected $300,000 in fees for city jobs, and had a $1 million hidden in a safe deposit box. Walker had no defense, except to charge that Seabury was a Communist.

Roosevelt, meanwhile, had his eye on the White House and needed Tammany support in his home state. He was faced with the choice of having Walker removed and risking the wrath of the machine, or letting him off the hook and inviting charges of cronyism from the Republican opposition. He steered a middle course and demanded that the Mayor explain himself. A day later, Jimmy Walker, always the gent, solved the Governor's problem by resigning. Then he sailed off for an extended trip to Europe. In any other city, it should have marked the end of the political machine. But New York held a special election and chose John P. O'Brien to succeed the fallen angel. When reporters asked the completely loyal Tammany man what his first act as mayor would be, O'Brien said, "I don't know, they haven't told me yet."

His epitaph might have been "he served his time." While he did, some influential New Yorkers were hard at work uniting among themselves to form a fusion party and find a candidate to carry their flag into battle in the next election. They found their man in Fiorello H. LaGuardia. On January 1, 1934, he became the ninety-ninth Mayor of New York, and the city hasn't been the same since.

Even before 1929, privation was a common sight on the Bowery (left), but for those outside the Stock Exchange (below left) at the time of the Crash, it was all tragically new.

Between 1914 and 1918, Florenz Ziegfeld brought his fabulous Follies, and Broadway's first five-dollar ticket price, to the Amsterdam Theater. And every pretty girl in town shared the dream of becoming a Follies Girl.

Overleaf: among the accomplishments of Mayor Fiorello LaGuardia and Robert Moses, his Parks Commissioner, Robert Moses, nothing quite compared to the 1939 World's Fair.

In 1919, the burlesque operators on Broadway began cleaning up their act by putting clothes on the girls, censoring the comedians' jokes and banning smoking in their theaters. Then they raised their prices. But their old customers weren't happy at all, and a New Yorker named Billy Minsky began giving them what they wanted, the same old stuff, but with a new innovation he called the "striptease." By 1928 he had the only game in town.

But if presenting comedians like Phil Silvers and Abbott and Costello added fun to the New York scene, Fiorello LaGuardia was not amused. On April 30, 1937, when Billy Minsky's license to operate six burlesque theaters expired, the Little Flower not only refused to renew it, but passed a law making it illegal to use the word "burlesque," not to mention banning the use of the name "Minsky" anywhere in his fair city. To protect their investment, the striptease operators changed their name to "Follies," but they didn't change their act.

"I HAVE SEEN THE FUTURE!"

The midpoint of the LaGuardia Administration, 1939, was also the 150th anniversary of George Washington's inauguration. Parks Commissioner Robert Moses, who was beating the drums for a greensward from one end of Queens to the other, had hit upon an idea that would provide the funds for making green a dump which was ironically called Flushing Meadows. The land had been bought by the city for a park years earlier, but a Tammany businessman named Fishhooks McCarthy had used it as the private dump for a Brooklyn garbage hauling company he owned. By the time Moses began to dream his dream, he said that the rats there were "big enough to wear saddles." A world's fair was his answer and it was an idea that perfectly suited the Mayor.

The memorial to George Washington, the peg, so to speak, that they had hung their hat on, was quickly relegated to an inconspicuous pavilion in the

N Y Worlds Fair 1939 Preview.

Amusement Area. The statue of the first President overlooked the Borden Building, one of the Fair's most popular attractions, in which 150 cows were tended and milked by a machine called a Rotolactor. However, the attraction of the 1939 New York World's Fair was the future. It was a time in New York's history when the recent past was too dreary to contemplate.

Of all the fairgoers who wore the buttons handed out by General Motors proclaiming, "I have seen the future," no one wore one with more enthusiasm than Fiorello H. LaGuardia. Transforming a dump into the City of Tomorrow had been a symbolic act, and it was clear to anyone who looked west that the skyline off in the distance represented a city with a future. The Fair provided an opportunity to show off a brand-new bridge connecting three of the five boroughs, and the

A one-time dump for a garbage hauling company owned by a Tammany businessman named Fishhooks McCarthy became the unlikely location for the City of Tomorrow that was the 1939 World's Fair. A second World's Fair was held there in 1964.

The symbol of the 1939 New York World's Fair was a 700-foot three-sided pylon, called the Trylon, attached to 200-foot-wide Perisphere, which contained a diorama of a city of the future called "Democracity."

CHAPTER 11

LaGuardia was swept into office on a promise to clean up the city. Even he didn't know what a big job it would be.

new highways to serve it. Before the Fair closed, at the end of the first of its two years of existence, LaGuardia had a permanent monument of his own not far away. On October 15, 1939, as the Mayor proudly watched, an American Airlines plane from Canada touched down on the runway of North Beach Airport. A month later, the Board of Estimate voted to rename it in honor of the Mayor and the following summer, as the first scheduled flight to Europe lifted off, the new name became official.

Of all his enthusiasms, LaGuardia loved flying best. He had gotten a pilot's license in 1915, and two years later, when the United States entered World War I, he went to Europe to join the war in the air. He had served a term in Congress by then, and, while he was away, he was overwhelmingly reelected. Even his Republican opposition found it necessary to sponsor a testimonial dinner in his honor, and in Manhattan's Little Italy, the

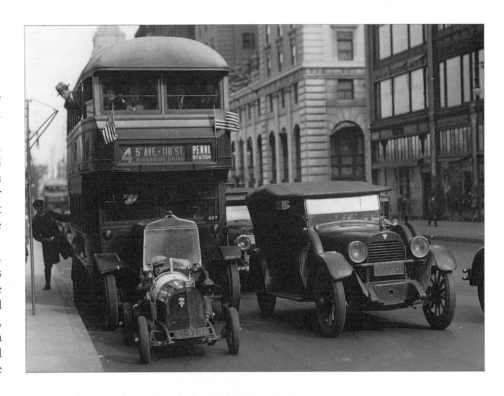

Cars, buses and trucks of every description were choking New York's streets by the 1930s, but a lot of die-hard delivery men still thought the best advice was "get a horse."

185

name Fiorello became the first choice at the christenings of baby boys.

After he became Mayor, he traveled some 38,000 miles by plane, but he was annoyed that his city didn't have an airport of its own. He made his feelings known when on a 1934 flight from Chicago which landed at Newark. "My ticket says Chicago to New York," he said, and he refused to get off the plane. They finally had to fly him to Floyd Bennett Field in Brooklyn. He had made his point and it didn't go unnoticed in Washington. He had already been barraging the Post Office Department with telegrams every time Newark was shut down by bad weather, pointing out that Floyd Bennett was open. After he landed there himself, regular mail runs followed him.

The Little Flower, as he was known, was a living symbol of New York. He was perceived as the son of an immigrant, born in the mean streets, who rose above his humble beginnings with a pugnacious can-do attitude. But his life story didn't quite fit the image.

Among the things the new Mayor eliminated were pushcart peddlers, and he pushed plans forward to improve the living conditions of their families, even though he had taken away their means of making a living.

Life on the Lower East Side hadn't changed much when LaGuardia moved into nearby City Hall. To many of the immigrants whose first experience of New York living was on the Lower East Side, however, even these cramped and rudimentary conditions must have seemed like heaven compared with what they had endured back home.

CHAPTER 11

Recovery from the Depression was slow, and well-dressed men continued supporting themselves by selling apples. But in spite of hard times and tight quotas, immigrants kept arriving at Ellis Island.

His father, Achille, had indeed emigrated from Italy, but he came from a moderately wealthy family and by the time he arrived in New York in 1878, he had traveled all over Europe as a bandmaster and composer. He spoke four languages fluently and had accumulated enough money to live in Greenwich Village, which he selected because of its European atmosphere. In 1885, when young Fiorello Enrico was three years old, Achille became the leader of an army band and moved his family to the territory that would one day become North Dakota. By the time Fiorello he was ready for school, they had moved to the shores of Lake Ontario in upstate New York. Eventually they moved on to Prescott, Arizona, which LaGuardia considered to be his home town. Later, when he would have licked any man in the house who challenged his love of New York, the Little Flower usually wore a reminder of his days in the Wild West: a high-brimmed cowboy hat.

But as Mayor he wore many hats. And the one he seemed to enjoy wearing most was a fireman's helmet.

Newly-arrived future Americans were carefully examined as possible typhus carriers, but putting food into their mouths was another problem.

New York City's firefighters never lacked for friends and loyal supporters, but Fiorello LaGuardia was the best friend and supporter the Department ever had.

Fiorello LaGuardia never lacked for friends or supporters, and he kept their enthusiasm alive through regular Sunday broadcasts on the city's station, WNYC.

The Fire Department installed an alarm bell in his office, and he responded to it as quickly as they did, appearing on the scene in his helmet and yellow slicker, and staying until the last sparks had disappeared. He answered police calls, too, and insisted on being in their front lines. "What would the men think if I didn't have the guts to go where they went?" he asked. In doing so he invented the photo opportunity, an institution modern politicians couldn't live without. He also found a communicational opportunity in movies,

Slum clearance and the beautification of New York were two of LaGuardia's many well-known works as Mayor. Organ grinders (facing page), however, were among his dislikes, so His Honor made them illegal. LaGuardia's long list of supporters included First Lady Eleanor Roosevelt (left).

When the Colonial mansion of Archibald Gracie was designated the official Mayor's residence in 1942, LaGuardia didn't want to move in because he thought it would look as though he'd gone "high hat."

and set up an office to encourage more location shooting on the sidewalks of New York. To reach still more of his constituents, he created a municipal radio station, WNYC, in 1939. Three years later, he began using the station for what he called his Sunday Sermons, a half-hour chat following the playing of the Marine hymn, which covered every topic that interested him, from the state of the World War to men he accused of being tinhorn politicians. It was estimated that twenty-five percent of the city's population tuned in to him every Sunday. Even today, some New Yorkers say they remember hearing the Mayor reading the Sunday funnies on the air. Actually, he only did it once, on July 1, 1945, during a newspaper strike.

Long before the Mayor moved into his fancy house on the East River, the old Lower East Side had been cleaned up at his insistence.

CHAPTER 11

The whole city had been transformed by the 1940s. The Police Department had become respectable and Fifth Avenue traffic, which had an almost genteel quality in the '20s and '30s, had become more aggressive.

LaGuardia, who enjoyed surprises, decided not to use his sermon that day to fill the news gap, but announced instead, "Gather 'round, children, and I will tell you about Dick Tracy." It was far and away the most popular of his radio hours, and he assigned the station's announcers to carry on reading the comics every day until the strike was over. He said that he would stay in the wings as a possible interpreter if it became necessary. But it didn't. The strike ended soon and, when the papers came back, *The Times* said the Little Flower's "flamboyances will be remembered long after his more solid accomplishments are forgotten."

When he moved into City Hall, LaGuardia said

Like other parts of the city, Forty-Second Street, too, had been transformed. The old Grand Central Depot had been replaced, and though the city still had streetcars, their days were numbered.

CHAPTER 11

New York had its eye on the future in the 1940s, and almost no one missed scenes like this that were common on the Lower East Side at the turn of the century.

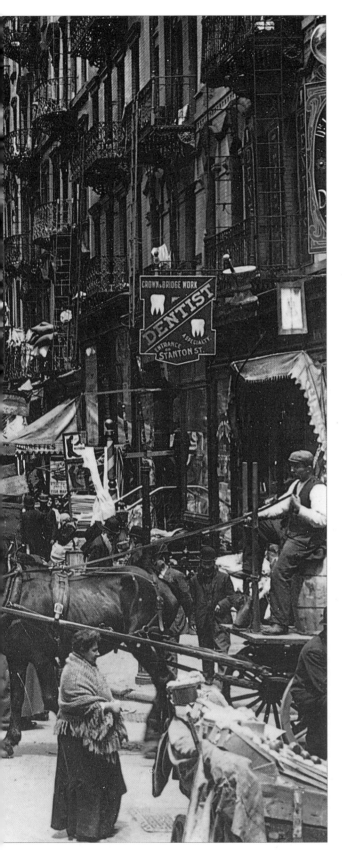

"There are people who like things as they are. I can't hold out any hope for them." One of the first signs that things would be different came on the day that one of the new Mayor's close friends found a police officer putting a ticket on his car. The friend tore his ticket in half and was instantly arrested. When his complaint reached City Hall, LaGuardia picked up the phone. The Precinct Captain who made the call in explanation protested that the officer involved was a rookie and didn't know better. "You idiot!," shouted the Mayor.

The Second Avenue Elevated vanished in 1942. Elevated trains on Sixth Avenue, which passed the Herald Building, stopped in 1938.

199

After cleaning up the Lower East Side (right), the Mayor took on the job of cooling tensions in Harlem that had erupted in rioting in 1943 (facing page, top). Meanwhile, Commissioner Moses, in his role of Chairman of the Triborough Bridge Authority, unveiled plans for a Battery-to-Brooklyn Bridge (facing page, bottom). LaGuardia was one of the few who thought it was a good idea.

"He may be a rookie, but he's a better cop than you are." That same morning, the Mayor's limousine delivered a box of cigars to the patrolman, and the Mayor's friend was told he was no longer welcome at City Hall.

Among his proudest accomplishments was eliminating street peddlers from the city's sidewalks and providing them with indoor markets to carry on their trade. In the process, he curbed the influence of racketeers who had terrorized their way into forming monopolies in just about every commodity, from fish to butter and eggs. Not all of them went away quietly. When the Mayor took off after Ciro Terranova, who controlled the sale of every artichoke in New York, the Artichoke King called on a civil rights organization to protect him. The Mayor backed down, but not for long. At the crack of dawn on the coldest day of the year,

CHAPTER 11

In the LaGuardia years,
Commissioner Moses built
hundreds of playgrounds
to make street scenes like
this a thing of the past.

LaGuardia showed up at the Bronx Terminal Market with a corps of buglers to announce his arrival. Once he had the attention of all the workers, he proceeded to read a proclamation which said that a law dating back to Dutch days allowed him to prohibit the sale of any type of food. It went on to say that he was hereby stopping the sale of artichokes. He didn't really have the power, but he did have a Federal order in his pocket that put Terranova out of business. That wouldn't have gotten any headlines, though, and His Honor wanted to make sure the people knew who was responsible when the price of artichokes dropped suddenly.

He demanded the best from all the people who worked for him and didn't mind showing them the door when they didn't deliver it. But of all the people who served him, the one whom most observers thought would soon be out on his ear was his Parks Commissioner, Robert Moses. The two men never stopped fighting in public, but though President

Highways, bridges, parks and beaches, all received close scrutiny from Robert Moses. He also built dozens of public swimming pools, which made dog-paddling in the harbor obsolete. ... And Rivington Street (below left), on the Lower East Side, would never look the same again.

When war came to Europe, New Yorkers became used to air raid drills and bomb shelters they hoped they'd never have to use for real.

Roosevelt was constantly threatening to cut LaGuardia from Federal funds if he didn't get rid of Moses, the Little Flower was one of his greatest supporters and, in the twelve years of the LaGuardia Administration, they built more parks than any other administration had done before or since. They built three major bridges and created fifty miles of highways. Moses's own estimate of LaGuardia's legacy to New York was unquestionably, "The public works. He stood up for them, and he has to get the credit." The Mayor privately called his Commissioner "His Grace," but he grudgingly admitted that "Robert Moses couldn't survive a Tammany administration for three good reasons: first, he knows his job; second, he is honest; third, he has opinions of his own." It could have been a good description of the Mayor himself.

During his last radio broadcast before retiring in 1945, LaGuardia read a letter from a boy who had sent

As kids fished coins from subway gratings, many adults recalled the time the dirigible Hindenburg flew over the city and wondered if Hitler would send another like it. The Mayor, meanwhile, stayed calm and contemplated the future of the Big Apple.

Overleaf: the tip of Lower Manhattan and the South Street piers in the '40s.

him eighteen cents to cover the cost of a light he had stolen from Central Park. It was signed "City Ruffian." Then the Little Flower leaned toward the microphone and in a soft voice said, "No, son, you are not a ruffian at all. You did the right thing. You are a good boy." It was the last public statement he made as Mayor and, to some, it summed up what New York loved best about Fiorello LaGuardia. After so many years of Good Old Boys in City Hall, he had showed them what a good boy could be worth.

LaGuardia led New York City out of the Great Depression and through the years of World War II. Most important, he planted a flower in New York and gave it a zest for the future. One of the men who had worked at his side said, "He could be cynical, churlish, hot-headed, petty and just plain wrong. At one time or another, he antagonized everyone who ever worked for him. But he also gave us all a standard of excellence, a sense of adventure in government, pride in what we were doing. He was actually making New York a better place to live. And he made us all part of the excitement."